Thailand Travel Guide: Typical Costs, Traveling, Accommodation, Culture, Sport, Bangkok, Banglamphu, Ratanakosin & Thonburi, Chiang Mai, Chiang Rai, Phuket & More

by Todd Wright

Contents

Introduction 13

Typical Costs.. 15

Money Saving Tips 17

Top Things to See and Do in Thailand 19

Facts 28

Getting there.. 29

    Flights from the UK and Ireland 29

    Flights from the US and Canada 30

    Flights from Australia and New Zealand 31

    Flights from South Africa 31

    Agents and operators... 32

    Travel via neighbouring countries........................... 34

    Burma.. 35

    Cambodia 35

    Laos and Vietnam 36

    Malaysia and Singapore 37

Getting around.. 39

    Inter-town buses 39

    Ordinary and second-class 40

    First-class and VIP 41

    Tickets and timetables... 42

    Songthaews, share-taxis and air-conditioned minibuses 43

    Trains 45

    Ferries... 48

    Flights... 49

Local transport 51

Buses and songthaews 51

Longtail boats 52

Taxi services 53

Tuk-tuks 54

Samlors 55

Motorbike taxis 56

Vehicle rental 58

Renting a car 60

Renting a motorbike 60

Cycling 62

Cycling practicalities 63

Hitching 64

Accommodation 65

Where to eat 67

How to eat 69

What to eat 70

Curries and soups 71

Salads 72

Noodle and rice dishes 73

Regional dishes 75

Desserts 76

Drinks 77

Alcoholic drinks 79

Culture and etiquette 81

The monarchy 81

Religion 82

The body 82

Social conventions 83

Thai names 84

The media 87

Newspapers and magazines 87

Television 88

Radio 88

Festivals 89

A festival calendar 89

Entertainment and sport 94

Drama and dance 94

Khon 94

Lakhon 96

Likay 96

Nang 97

Film 98

Thai boxing 99

Takraw 101

Spas and traditional massage 103

Meditation centres and retreats 105

Meditation centres and retreat temples 107

Outdoor activities 109

Diving and snorkelling 109

Diving 110

Trips and courses 111

Snorkelling 112

National parks and wildlife observation 112

Rock climbing 113

Sea kayaking and whitewater rafting 113

Trekking 114

Travelling with children 120

Hotels and transport 121

Other practicalities 121

Hazards 122

Information and advice 123

Travel essentials 124

Charities and volunteer projects 124

Climate 126

Costs 126

Crime and personal safety 128

Theft 128

Personal safety 129

Regional issues 130

Scams 131

Age restrictions and other laws 132

Drugs 133

Customs regulations 134

Departure taxes 135

Electricity 135

Entry requirements 135

Border runs, extensions and re-entry permits 137

Thai embassies and consulates abroad 138

Gay and lesbian Thailand...140

The scene..141

Information and contacts for gay travellers....................141

Health 143

Inoculations 144

Mosquito-borne diseases 144

Malaria 145

Dengue fever 146

Rabies...146

Other bites and stings 146

Worms and flukes 148

Digestive problems..148

HIV and AIDS...149

Medical resources...149

Insurance 150

Other basics..151

Internet 151

Laundry 151

Left luggage 151

Living in Thailand...152

Study, work and volunteer programmes.........................152

Mail 153

Maps..154

Money and banks 155

Opening hours and public holidays................................157

National holidays 157

Phones 158

Photography 159

Time 160

Tipping 160

Tourist information 160

TAT offices abroad 161

Travellers with disabilities 161

When to go 163

Experiences in Thailand 165

Bangkok 165

Full-on Food 165

Fun Folks 166

Urban Exploration 166

Contrasts 167

Experiences in Bangkok 169

Siam Square, Pratunam, Ploenchit & Ratchathewi 169

Jim Thompson House 169

MBK Center 171

Baan Khrua 173

Erawan Shrine 174

Banglamphu 177

Experiences in Banglamphu 177

Golden Mount 177

Krua Apsorn 178

Brick Bar 179

Wat Suthat...180

Northern Bangkok...183

Experiences in Northern Bangkok 183

Chatuchak Weekend Market 183

Chang Chui 186

Route 66 187

Nonthaburi Market 189

Ko Ratanakosin & Thonburi 191

Experiences in Ko Ratanakosin & Thonburi.........191

Wat Pho...191

Wat Phra Kaew 193

Wat Arun...195

Amulet Market 197

Riverside, Silom & Lumphini 200

Experiences in Riverside, Silom & Lumphini.........200

Nahm...200

Moon Bar 201

Lumpini Park...202

Chaophraya Cruise 204

Chinatown 205

Experiences in Chinatown....................................205

Nay Hong 205

Wat Traimit (Golden Buddha) 206

Talat Mai 207

Talat Noi 209

Phahurat 210

Chiang Mai...213

   Experiences in Chiang Mai 213

   Wat Phra That Doi Suthep 213

   Wat Phra Singh 215

   Saturday Walking Street 217

   Talat Pratu Chiang Mai 218

   Riverside Bar & Restaurant...............................219

   Lanna Folklife Museum 220

   Wat U Mong...222

Railay 225

Chiang Rai Province 226

   Sights in Chiang Rai Province 226

   Mae Fah Luang Art & Culture Park..................226

   Wat Rong Khun..227

   Baandam..229

Ayutthaya 231

   Sights in Ayuthaya 231

   Wat Ratchaburana 231

   Wat Phra Si Sanphet..233

   Wat Mahathat 234

Kanchanaburi 237

   Sights in Kanchanaburi 237

   Death Railway Bridge..237

   Thailand–Burma Railway Centre......................239

   Wat Tham Seua 240

Similan Islands Marine National Park 242

Sights in Similan Islands Marine National Park 242

Ko Tachai 242

Ko Bon 243

Hin Pousar 244

Pai 246

Sights in Pai 246

Ban Santichon 246

Wat Phra That Mae Yen 247

Nam Tok Mo Paeng 249

Phuket 250

Sights in Phuket 250

Big Buddha 250

Laem Phromthep 252

Hat Bang Thao 253

Pha Taem National Park 253

Conclusion 255

THAILAND

Introduction

With sixteen million foreigners flying into the country each year, Thailand is Asia's primary travel destination and offers a host of places to visit. Yet despite this vast influx of visitors, Thailand's cultural integrity remains largely undamaged – a country that adroitly avoided colonization has been able to absorb Western influences while maintaining its own rich heritage. Though the high-rises and neon lights occupy the foreground of the tourist picture, the typical Thai community is still the farming village, and you need not venture far to encounter a more traditional scene of fishing communities, rubber plantations and Buddhist temples. Around forty percent of Thais earn their living from the land, based around the staple rice, which forms the foundation of the country's unique and famously sophisticated cuisine.

Tourism has been just one factor in the country's development which, since the deep-seated uncertainties surrounding the Vietnam War faded, has been free, for the most part, to proceed at death-defying pace – for a time in the 1980s and early 1990s, Thailand boasted the fastest-expanding economy in the world. Politics in Thailand, however, has not been able to keep pace. Since World War II, coups d'état have been as common a method of changing government as general elections; the malnourished democratic system – when the armed forces allow it to operate – is characterized by corruption and cronyism.

Through all the changes of the last sixty years, the much-revered constitutional monarch, King Bhumibol, who sits at the pinnacle of an elaborate hierarchical system of deference covering the whole of Thai society, has lent a measure of stability. Furthermore, some 85 percent of the population are still practising Theravada Buddhists, a unifying faith that colours all aspects of daily life – from the tiered temple rooftops that dominate every skyline, to the omnipresent saffron-robed monks and the packed calendar of festivals.

Thailand is the travel hub of Southeast Asia. Most people coming into the region fly into Bangkok and make that their base for doing the circuit around Southeast Asia. With its lush jungles, famed beaches, world-class diving, amazing food, friendly and cheap prices, Thailand is by far my favorite country in the world! I've been coming to the country since 2005, lived there for 2 years, and always seem pulled back to it. It's an easy country to travel and you can meet a lot of other people there. You're never alone! The country is a well-worn destination on the backpacking trail and everything is convenient and easy. However, there are still many off the beaten path destinations aways from the crowds and the prices they bring. Overall, Thailand speaks for itself. When you hear its name, you already think about beaches, beauty, jungles, and food. And your thoughts are spot on.

Typical Costs

Accommodation – Thailand is very cheap, though the north is far cheaper than Bangkok and the southern islands. You can find cheap guesthouses for as little 300 THB per night in cities and 200 THB per night in the countryside, though in the big cities like Chiang Mai and Bangkok, rooms start at about 400 per night. On the islands or for a nicer room with air-conditioner, expect to pay 600 THB and up per night. Basic bungalows cost the same. Hotels start at around 1,350 THB per night and go up from there. Big resorts on the islands start at 1,700 THB per night for a bungalow on the beach. Dorm rooms, which are increasingly widespread throughout the country, range from 100-150 THB per night.Airbnb is also growing in Thailand and a good amount of cities have a nice selection. A shared room starts around 350 THB per night and renting a full apartment starts around 700 THB per night. Chada Guesthouse (Bangkok), Julies (Chiang Mai), Kodchasri B&B (Chiang Mai), Pooh's (Ko Lipe), Greenhouse (Khao Yai) are my favorite places to sleep in the country.

Food – Food is really cheap in Thailand. Street food costs as little as 20 THB, though on average you'll spend about 35-50 THB per meal if you want something really filling. If you stick to the local street food, you can eat for around 120-170 THB a day. Most western dishes (burgers, pizza, pasta, etc) cost between 170-340 THB, though they can be higher in the fancier western establishments. Since food is so cheap, there's no point in grocery shopping unless you're looking to get some pre-made salads or fruits. Visit each city guide for specific food recommendations in each place!

Transportation – Like everything in Thailand, transportation is also cheap. Local buses cost as little as 8 THB per trip, the Metro and Skytrain in Bangkok cost 15-50 THB per trip and metered taxi rides are usually 60-100 THB each. Tuk-tuks are un-metered and generally more expensive, costing 100-235 THB per ride. Motorbike taxis (in orange vests) are available all over the country with short trips costing about 35 THB (you need to negotiate the price). Train service around the country is cheap – day trains cost as little as 50 THB. Night trains start at 575 THB for second-class without air-conditioning. Boats to/from the islands cost between 250-475 THB. (Note: It's often better to get a bus/boat package then pay for them separately.) Coach buses are a great way to get around the country. For example, a bus ride from Bangkok to Chiang Mai costs 550-700 THB and a bus ride from Bangkok to Phuket costs 500-1,000 THB.

Activities – Day tours cost 500-1,200 THB depending on the activity. Jungle trekking costs 1,000-1,685 THB per day. Keep in mind, you have more bargaining power if you go with a group. Most parks and national museums cost between 50-100 THB to get into (as a non-Thai, you'll always pay a higher rate). A PADI dive certification course (very popular in Thailand) costs around 10,000 THB (but often includes accommodation).

Suggested daily budget – 900-1080 THB / 25-30 USD (Note: This is a suggested budget assuming you're staying in a hostel, eating out a little, cooking most of your meals or eating cheap street food, and using local transportation. Using the budget tips below, you can always lower this number. However, if you stay in fancier accommodation or eat out more often, expect this to be higher!)

Money Saving Tips

Go local – The easiest way to save money in Thailand is to simply live like a local. Take local buses, eat street food, and drink local beer. The average Thai lives on a less than 7,750 THB per month in Bangkok, and on even less in the country side. If you stay at cheap guesthouses and eat street food, you can spend as little as 335 THB per day.

Eat street food – Speaking of street food, don't be afraid to eat it. It's safe — sometimes it's even safer than restaurant food. If it wasn't, Thai people wouldn't be packed in the food stalls each day. You'll find the best of Thailand's food on the street and it will cost you a fraction of what you pay at a restaurant.

Buy beer at 7-Eleven – Buying beer at Thailand's ubiquitous 7-Elevens and drinking outside will save you quite a bit on your bar tab. A beer in

7-Eleven is about 35 THB, while the same beer will cost 100-170 THB in a restaurant or bar.

Take advantage of happy hour – Thailand's many happy hours have half-priced drinks and 2-for-1 specials.

Don't book any tours before you arrive – Want to take a cooking class? Go zip-lining? Trek in the jungle? Dive? Wait until you get into Thailand to book anything. Travel agencies are located all over the tourist areas, looking to sell their tours. Time to brush up on your negotiation skills. You're able to purchase these tours online before you arrive, but you'll be paying a lot more!

Stay in hostels – Hostels are both an economical and social choice for Thailand. There are tons to chose from, especially in the really touristy areas of Thailand. Bring some earplugs and prepare to save a lot of money!

Couchsurf — Nothing's cheaper than sleeping for free. Couchsurfing connects you with locals who will give you not only a free place to stay, but also a local tour guide who can introduce you to all the great places to see.

Top Things to See and Do in Thailand

Explore Bangkok – The heart of Thailand, this crazy city is a must-see. Most travelers don't like it right away but it grows on you. Explore temples, palaces, amazing markets, shops, one of the craziest nightlife scenes in the world, and of course, amazing Thai food. At first, I didn't like this place but now it's one of the places I feel most at home in. I love this city and return frequently.

Visit the Grand Palace and Wat Pho – Thailand's royal palace was built at the end of the 18th century by King Rama I and is the official residence of the current monarch (though he doesn't live there anymore; now it's just used for ceremonies). It's a striking place filled with numerous temples, including Wat Pra Kaeo, which houses the 15th-century Emerald Buddha. Nearby Wat Pho is famous for two things: a larger-than-life golden reclining Buddha statue and a very relaxing massage school.

Find adventure around Chiang Mai – Chiang Mai is an old city ringed with temples and surrounded by jungles. It's a good launching pad for jungle treks into the area; there is a nearby elephant sanctuary, and the Chiang Mai night market is a place for some of the best handicrafts and deals in the country.

Hike in Khao Yai National Park – Khao Yai National Park located about 2.5 hours north of Bangkok and is one of Thailand's best national parks. It's truly amazing — visually stunning, empty of tourists, and filled with lush flora and fauna and even a few wild elephants. This park is an excellent place to hike and swim. It's not very crowded so you'll have the jungle to yourself. Stay at the Greenleaf Guesthouse for the best tour/accommodation deals in the area. Park entrance costs 400 THB.

Visit Khao Sok National Park – Located in the south of Thailand, Khao Sok National Park is constantly rated as one of the best in Thailand, with incredible trekking, camping, limestone karsts, cooling rivers, and a glistening lake. You'll find semi-challenging hikes, tons of wildlife, walking paths, and incredible sunsets. Park entrance costs 200 THB.

Hop around the ancient capitals – Between Chiang Mai and Bangkok are Thailand's three ancient capitals – Sukhothai, Lopburi, and Ayutthaya. Visiting them on your way north is a unique way to head from Bangkok to Chiang Mai. You'll get to learn about ancient Thailand and see rural life at its best. My favorite is Ayutthaya.

Relax on tropical islands – Thailand has a million and one beautiful tropical islands. Some are overdeveloped, while others only have a single bungalow on them. You'll find everything here. Some of the best islands here are – Ko Samet, Ko Taruato, Ko Lanta, Ko Chang, Ko Tao, Ko Jum, Ko Lipe, Ko Phi Phi, Phuket, the Similan Islands, and Ko Samui.

Partake in the Full Moon Party – If you like partying, there's no better party in the world than the famous Full Moon Party. The Full Moon

Party is a giant festival-like party with a lot of drinking, dancing, and drugs. Each bar has its own sound system, so you'll hear different music loudly blasting onto the beach every few feet. The beach itself is lined with people selling alcohol, fire dancers putting on shows, and little booths selling glow-in-the-dark face paint. Sure, it is super touristy but that doesn't mean it's not a lot of fun and it's as much a part of Thailand as anything else.

Go jungle trekking – There are some great jungle trekking opportunities in northern Thailand. Be sure to go on a multi-day hike. The shorter hikes aren't as good and the hill tribes you visit are like visiting a rural impoverished Disney World. The biggest departure points are Chiang Mai and Chiang Rai. Don't book any tours ahead of time, you can book these sorts of outings through the hostel or hostel you're staying in closeby. If you book online ahead of time, you will pay more.

Go scuba diving in the Similan Islands – Scuba diving here is a popular activity because of the crystal clear waters and majestic sea life. The cheapest place to learn is on the island of Ko Tao, which caters specifically for dive trips. Most people don't go unless they're planning on diving. While you can dive all over the country, the Similan Islands offer the best diving. If you dive the Similan Islands, be sure to see Elephant Head Rock, and the reef houses plenty of fish, snappers, rays, and turtles. Day trips start at 3,700 THB.

Learn to cook – Thai food is delicious and it's relatively easy to cook. All over the country, you'll find places to teach you, though the best are in Chiang Mai and Bangkok. Even if you don't plan to cook back home, at least you get to spend a day making and eating scrumptious food.

Explore the Khmer temples in Isaan – There are many temples built throughout the region, all along the ancient roads connecting Angkor to the other villages. The largest of these is Phimai, located at the end of the ancient highway. In the Buriram province are two other magnificent

Khmer temples only a few kilometers apart. Phanom Rung built on top of a hill and Muang Tum which is at the base of the hill.

Get off the trail in Isaan – One of the most under visited areas of the country, Isaan is mostly a land of farms and villages. This is a great place to escape the frantic tourist atmosphere of the rest of the country. It is not overrun by tourists, and you get a chance to experience Thai culture in a different, more personal way. I think it's one of the most interesting places in the country.

Take the day train – Taking the day train from Bangkok to Chiang Mai is not only cheaper but a much better way to see the countryside than the night train. Sure, you waste a day but you see the countryside, you experience how Thais take the train, and you're treated to vendors coming off and on every stop selling meals for 15 THB. The day trip remains one of my favorite experiences in Thailand. Just make sure you have a good book!

Throw water during Songkran – Between April 13-15th, the Thai celebrate Thai New Year by holding an enormous, three-day water fight. Songkran, as it's known, is meant to wash away the old and begin the year anew. It's an amazing festival and an unforgettable experience! Be prepared to get wet everywhere you go those days (and keep your electronics sealed in plastic).

Help the elephants at the Elephant Nature Park – Sure you can come to Thailand and ride an elephant, but so many of them in this country suffer from abuse. An even better way to get up-close-and-personal to the animals is to volunteer at the Elephant Conservation Center near Chiang Mai. A one-day visit costs 2,500 THB for adults.

Admire Wat Doi Suthep – This stunning Buddhist temples lies in Doi Suthep-Pui National Park, 10 miles out of Chiang Mai. A tram or a trek up 300 steps will take you to the summit of Doi Suthep, where the glittering gold temple spire awaits you. The temple dates back to the 14th century and holds rare relics of Buddha. It's really is too beautiful of a view to miss, so don't leave Chiang Mai without visiting Wat Doi Suthep. Admission is 30 THB. It's open from 6am-6pm.

Visit the Golden Triangle – The point where the Mekong River meets the Ruak River is known as the Golden Triangle. You can take a boat and head to the Golden Triangle Park, or check out some of the many Buddha statues and markets.

Phuket – This island is the biggest destination for tourism in Thailand. You'll find great beaches and amazing activities this island, and if you stay away from Patong Beach, you can avoid most of the over-development and crowds. Phuket draws a lot of tourists, and if you really want to enjoy the area, get out of the main spots.

Ko Phi Phi – This is one of the most popular tourist islands in Thailand. From the famous of Maya Bay (made famous in The Beach) to the monkeys on the aptly named Monkey Beach to the diving and nightlife, there are reasons people flock here. Destroyed by the tsunami in 2004, the island has been rebuilt and developed to an even greater extent than before.

Ko Lipe – Located in southern Thailand, this semi-off the map island is one of my favorite places in the world. Here on Ko Lipe, the super friendly locals bring in the daily catch for amazing seafood. The beaches are beautiful, the water warm, and the island cheap. I came for three days and then lived here for a month. In the last few years, it has become very developed and it's not the sleepy little island it used to be but it's still way less developed than many other destinations in Thailand. Moreover, you're near a pristine and undeveloped national marine park where you can snorkel and enjoy some beaches to yourself!

Shop at the floating markets – Thailand is full of markets. Perhaps the most whimsical of these are the floating markets, which can be found throughout the country. Some of the best are Damnoen Saduak, in Ratchaburi, and the Taling Chan Weekend Floating Market in Bangkok. You'll find rickety boats piled high with colorful goods and eats. You'll get plenty of great photos! (Although it's become majorly touristy to go to the floating markets, you'll not want to miss a morning shopping from boat to boat.)

Backpack through the Kanchanaburi Province – Here you'll find a lush forest perfect for trekking, though the history of this area is rather dark. The infamous Death Railway is located here, linking Burma and Myanmar, which were constructed during WWII by prisoners of war. This is also where you will find the Bridge on the River Kwai, built using POW labor and the subject of a both a film and a book. While it is a haunting reminder, it is an essential part of Thailand's history.

Motorbike through Northern Thailand – Around the Chiang Mai and Chiang Rai areas, there are lots of great routes. Many people rent bikes and tour the scenery. You can take a day trip, or you can take a couple of days – whatever suits your schedule. The Mai Hong Son Province offers a great loop that you can do starting in Chiang Mai and ending in Pai. Note: Make sure if you're renting a motorbike, you're comfortable with driving it and never (ever) drink and drive.

Relax in Pai – Pai has grown as a tourist destination in more recent years, but it is still a great place to escape some of the craziness of your larger cities. It is a true backpackers town, located in Northern Thailand. It is nestled in rolling green mountains and surrounded by waterfalls and incredible hiking trails. Be sure to take a day trip to the Tham Lot Caves, where you can take a stop off to swim in waterfalls and hot springs on your way there. Stay on the outskirts town in a lovely little bungalow, rent a bike, traverse the hills, and bathe in the cool waterfalls.

Facts

• Divided into 77 provinces or changwat, Thailand was known as Siam until 1939 (and again from 1945 to 1949); some academics suggest changing the name back again, to better reflect the country's Thai and non-Thai diversity.

• The population of 63 million is made up of ethnic Thais (75 percent) and Chinese (14 percent), with the rest comprising mainly immigrants from neighbouring countries as well as hill-tribespeople.

• Buddhism is the national religion, Islam the largest minority religion, but nearly all Thais also practise some form of animism (spirit worship).

• Since 1932 the country has been a constitutional monarchy. King Bhumibol, also known as Rama IX (being the ninth ruler of the Chakri dynasty), is the world's longest-ruling head of state, having been on the throne since 1946; the current prime minister, Yingluck Shinawatra, entered politics only six weeks before winning the general election in 2011 with an absolute majority.

• Thailand fell to 153rd out of 178 countries on Reporters without Borders' index on press freedom in 2010, because of a surge in the use of the lese-majesty laws.

• The world record for nonstop kissing was set by two Thai men in Pattaya on Valentine's Day, 2012, at a gobsmacking 50 hours, 25 minutes and 1 second.

Getting there

Thailand currently has six international airports, in Bangkok, Chiang Mai, Hat Yai, Krabi, Phuket and Ko Samui. The vast majority of travellers fly into Bangkok's Suvarnabhumi Airport.

Air fares to Thailand generally depend on the season, with the highest being approximately mid-November to mid-February, when the weather is best (with premium rates charged for flights between mid-Dec and New Year), and in July and August to coincide with school holidays. You will need to book several months in advance to get reasonably priced tickets during these peak periods.

The cheapest way of getting to most regional Thai airports is usually to buy a flight to Bangkok and then a separate domestic ticket (see Train information and booking). However, there are dozens of potentially useful, mostly seasonal, international routes into Phuket, including direct flights with several airlines from Australia. For Ko Samui, there are flights from Singapore, Hong Kong (both Bangkok Airways) and Kuala Lumpur (Berjaya Airlines and Firefly); for Krabi you can fly from KL with Air Asia, from Singapore with Tiger Airways or nonstop on seasonal, mostly charter flights from Scandinavia; and for Chiang Mai, Silk Air fly from Singapore, Air Asia from KL and Macau, while Korean Airlines from Seoul is a popular route for North American visitors.

Flights from the UK and Ireland

The fastest and most comfortable way of reaching Thailand from the UK is to fly nonstop from London to Bangkok with Qantas (wqantas.com.au), British Airways (wba.com), Thai Airways (wthaiair.com) or Eva Airways (wevaair.com), a journey of about eleven and a half hours. These airlines sometimes have special promotions, but a typical fare in high season might come in at around £900. Fares on indirect scheduled flights to Bangkok are always cheaper than nonstop flights – about £600 in high season if booked well in advance with Qatar Airways (wqatarairways.com), for example – though these journeys can take anything from two to twelve hours longer.

There are no nonstop flights from any regional airports in Britain or from any Irish airports, and rather than routing via London, you may find it convenient to fly to another hub such as Frankfurt (with Lufthansa; wlufthansa.com), Zurich (with Swiss; wswiss.com), Abu Dhabi (with Etihad; wetihadairways.com) or Dubai (with Emirates; wemirates.com), and take a connecting flight from there. Return flights from Newcastle upon Tyne with Emirates, for example, currently start at around £675 in high season, from Dublin via Copenhagen with SAS (wflysas.com), at around €800.

Flights from the US and Canada

Thai Airways (wthaiair.com) offers convenient flights from LA to Bangkok, with a one-hour stop in Seoul, charging around US$1600 in high season. Plenty of other airlines run to Bangkok from East and West Coast cities with one stop en route; it's generally easier to find a reasonable fare on flights via Asia than via Europe, even if you're departing from the East Coast. From New York, expect to pay upwards of US$1375 return in high season, including taxes, US$1250 from LA. Air Canada (waircanada.com) has the most convenient service to Bangkok from the largest number of Canadian cities; from Vancouver, expect to pay from around Can$1450 in high season; from Toronto, Can$1675. Cheaper rates are often available if you're prepared to make two or three stops and take more time.

Minimum flying times are twenty hours from New York or Toronto (westbound or eastbound), including stopovers, seventeen hours (nonstop) or nineteen and a half hours (with one stop) from LA, and eighteen hours from Vancouver.

Flights from Australia and New Zealand

There's no shortage of scheduled flights to Bangkok from Australia, with direct services from major cities operated by Thai Airways (wthaiair.com), Qantas (wqantas.com.au) and half a dozen others (around nine hours from Sydney and Perth), and plenty of indirect flights via Asian hubs, which take at least eleven and a half hours. You can also fly nonstop to Phuket from Sydney (with Jetstar; wjetstar.com) and Perth (on Thai and Virgin Australia; wvirginaustralia.com). There's often not much difference between the fares on nonstop and indirect flights with the major carriers, nor between the fares from the major eastern cities. From Sydney, if you book far in advance, you should be able to get a ticket to Bangkok in high season for around Aus$900, on a low-cost carrier such as Jetstar or through a special promotion with one of the major airlines; nonstop flights with the major airlines more typically cost around Aus$1200. Fares from Perth and Darwin are up to Aus$200 cheaper.

From New Zealand, Thai Airways runs nonstop twelve-hour flights between Auckland and Bangkok, costing from around NZ$1700 (including taxes) in high season. British Airways/Qantas flights from Auckland make brief stops in Sydney, adding about three hours to the trip, and other major Asian airlines offer indirect flights via their hubs (from 13hr, but more typically 17hr): fares for indirect flights can start as low as NZ$1500 in high season.

Flights from South Africa

From South Africa, Thai Airways (wthaiair.com), code-sharing with South African Airways (wflysaa.com), currently operate three nonstop flights a week from Johannesburg to Bangkok, taking eleven and a half hours and costing from around ZAR9,500 return for an advance booking in high season, including taxes. Otherwise, you'll be making a stop either in the Middle East or in Hong Kong or Southeast Asia, with fares starting at around ZAR8000 in high season.

Agents and operators

Adventure Center US t1-800/228-8747, wadventurecenter.com. Hiking and "soft adventure" specialist agent, offering dozens of packages to Thailand with well-regarded tour operators from all over the world.

All Points East UK t023/9225 8859, Thailand t081 885 9490; wallpointseast.com. Southeast Asia specialist operating small-group adventure holidays with off-the-beaten-track itineraries.

Andaman Discoveries Thailand wandamandiscoveries.com. Village-based homestay community tourism programmes around Khuraburi on the north Andaman coast, lasting from one to five days, which allow visitors to experience daily activities such as soap making, cashew-nut farming and roof thatching. Other tours include four-day trips to Ko Surin National Park to learn about Moken life.

Asian Trails Thailand wasiantrails.net. Well-regarded company that offers self-drive tours, cycling adventures, homestay programmes, river and sea cruises, plus more typical package tours.

Creative Events Asia Thailand wcreativeeventsasia.com. Wedding specialists for everything from paperwork to the ceremony and guest accommodation.

Crooked Trails US t206/383-9828, wcrookedtrails.com. Not-for-profit community-based tourism organization offering homestays along the Andaman coast, featuring volunteer work as well as cultural tours.

Eastern & Oriental Express UK t0845 077 2222, US t1-800/524 2420; worient-express.com. Tours by luxury train between Bangkok and Singapore, as well as to northern and northeastern Thailand.

ETC (Educational Travel Centre) Thailand wetc.co.th. Unusual tour programmes including Thai cooking holidays, rice-barge cruises to Ayutthaya, and community-based programmes and homestays that might include trekking and teaching.

Flight Centre Australia t13 31 33, Canada t1-877/967 5302, New Zealand t0800/243 544, South Africa t0860 400 727, UK t0870/499 0040, US t1-877/992 4732; wflightcentre.com. Guarantees to offer the lowest international air fares.

Grasshopper Adventures Australia t03/9016 3172, Thailand t02 280 0832, UK t020/8123 8144, US t818/921-7101; wgrasshopperadventures.com. Cycling day-tours around Bangkok, longer rides to Kanchanaburi and Ko Samui, and around Chiang Mai.

Intrepid Travel Australia t1300/018 871, Canada t1-866/360-1151, Ireland t01/524 0071, New Zealand t0800/600 610, South Africa t087 985 2798, UK t0800 781 1660, US t1-800/970 7299; wintrepidtravel.com. Well-regarded, small-group, off-the-beaten-track tour operator that offers over sixty trips to Thailand.

North South Travel UK t01245/608 291, wnorthsouthtravel.co.uk. Friendly, competitive travel agency, offering discounted fares worldwide. Profits are used to support projects in the developing world, especially the promotion of sustainable tourism.

Origin Asia Thailand walex-kerr.com. Cultural programmes that teach and explain living Thai arts such as dance, music, martial arts, textiles, flower offerings and cooking. Courses last from one day to a week and are held in Bangkok and Chiang Mai.

Responsible Travel UK t01273/600030, wresponsibletravel.com. One-stop shop for scores of fair-trade, ethically inclined holidays in Thailand, including trips that focus on wildlife, meditation, family activities and village life.

Spice Roads Thailand wspiceroads.com. Escorted bike tours through north, central and southern Thailand.

STA Travel Australia t134 782, New Zealand t0800/474 400, South Africa t0861/781 781, Thailand t02 236 0262, UK t0871/230/0040, US t1-800/781-4040; wstatravel.com. Worldwide specialists in independent travel. Good discounts for students and under-26s.

Symbiosis UK t0845/123 2844, wsymbiosis-travel.com. Upmarket, off-the-beaten-track tours with an environmentally sensitive, fair-trade focus, including visiting hill tribes by mountain bike, and kayaking at Khao Sok and Ko Tarutao.

Telltale Travel UK t0800/011 2571, wtelltaletravel.co.uk. Tailor-made, upscale company that offers off-the-beaten-track wildlife, cultural, family, cooking and well-being tours, as well as group trips for solo travellers.

Thailand Birdwatching Thailand wthailandbirdwatching.com. Specialist birdwatching tours in national parks and nature reserves.

Trailfinders UK t0845 058 5858, Ireland t01 677 7888; wtrailfinders.com. One of the best-informed and most efficient agents for independent travellers, with 24 branches in Britain and Ireland.

Travel Cuts Canada t1-800/667 2887, US t1-800/592-2887; wtravelcuts.com. Popular, long-established specialists in budget travel, including student and youth discount offers.

USIT Australia t1800 092499, Ireland t01/602 1906; wusit.ie. Ireland's main outlet for discounted, youth and student fares, with a branch in Sydney.

Travel via neighbouring countries

Sharing land borders with Burma, Laos, Cambodia and Malaysia, Thailand works well as part of many overland itineraries, both across

Asia and between Europe and Australia. Bangkok is also one of the major regional flight hubs for Southeast Asia.

The main restrictions on overland routes in and out of Thailand are determined by where the permitted land crossings lie and by visas. Details of visa requirements for travel to Thailand's immediate neighbours are outlined below, but should be double-checked before you travel. All Asian embassies are located in Bangkok (see Gem scams), but waiting times can be shorter at visa-issuing consulates outside the capital: China and India run consulates in Chiang Mai, and Laos and Vietnam have consulates in Khon Kaen. In Bangkok, many Khao San tour agents offer to get your visa for you, but beware: some are reportedly faking the stamps, which could get you into pretty serious trouble, so it's safer to go to the embassy yourself.

The right paperwork is also crucial if you're planning to drive your own car or motorbike into Thailand; see the Golden Triangle Rider website (wgt-rider.com) for advice.

Burma

There is no overland access from Burma (Myanmar) into Thailand and access in the opposite direction is restricted. Western tourists are only allowed to make limited-distance trips into Burma, usually just for the day, at Thachileik opposite Mae Sai, at Myawaddy near Mae Sot, and at Kaw Thaung (Victoria Point) near Ranong. The crossing at Three Pagodas Pass near Kanchanaburi is currently open only to Thai tourists. At these borders you generally enter Burma on a temporary US$10 (or B500) visa and then get a new fifteen-day visa when returning to Thailand; see relevant accounts for details.

Cambodia

At the time of writing, six overland crossings on the Thai–Cambodia border are open to non-Thais. See the relevant town accounts for specific details on all the border crossings; for travellers' up-to-the-minute experiences, plus an account of the common scam on through-transport from Bangkok to Siem Reap, consult wtalesofasia.com/cambodia-overland.htm.

Most travellers use either the crossing at Poipet, which has transport connections to Sisophon, Siem Reap and Phnom Penh and lies just across the border from the Thai town of Aranyaprathet, with its transport to Bangkok and, with a change in Sa Kaew, to Chanthaburi; or they follow the route from Sihanoukville in Cambodia via Koh Kong and Hat Lek to Trat, which is near Ko Chang on Thailand's east coast.

The crossings in northeast Thailand include the Chong Chom–O'Smach border pass, near Kap Choeng in Thailand's Surin province (see Crossing the Cambodian border via Chong Chom), and the Sa Ngam–Choam border in Si Saket province; from both these borders there's transport to Anlong Veng and Siem Reap. There are also two crossings in Chanthaburi province, with transport to and from Pailin in Cambodia.

Thirty-day tourist visas for Cambodia are issued to travellers on arrival at Phnom Penh and Siem Reap airports, and at all the above-listed land borders; you need US$20 and one photo for this. If you want to buy an advance thirty-day visa, you can do so online at wmfaic.gov.kh/evisa which takes three working days and costs US$25; these "e-visas" can only be used at the international airports and at Poipet and Ko Kong land borders, but might help you to avoid the more excessive scams at the land borders.

Laos and Vietnam

There are five main points along the Lao border where tourists can cross into Thailand: Houayxai (for Chiang Khong); Vientiane (for Nong Khai); Khammouan (aka Thakhek, for Nakhon Phanom); Savannakhet (for Mukdahan); and Pakse (for Chong Mek). All these borders can also be used as exits into Laos; see relevant town account for transport details.

Visas are required for all non-Thai visitors to Laos. A thirty-day visa on arrival can be bought for US$30–42 (depending on your nationality), plus one photo, at Vientiane, Luang Prabang and Pakse airports, and all the above-listed land borders. Or you can buy one in advance from either the Lao Embassy in Bangkok or the Lao Consulate in Khon Kaen for about the same fee.

It's possible to travel from Vietnam to Thailand via Savannakhet on the Lao–Thai border in a matter of hours; you'll need to use Vietnam's Lao Bao border crossing, west of Dong Ha, where you can catch a bus to Savannakhet and then another bus across the Mekong bridge to Mukdahan. All travellers into Vietnam need to buy a visa in advance. Thirty-day visas can take up to four working days to process at the embassy in Bangkok and cost from around B1000, depending on nationality (much more for same- or next-day processing); processing is usually quicker at the Vietnamese consulate in Khon Kaen.

Malaysia and Singapore

Travelling between Thailand and Malaysia and Singapore has in the past been a straightforward and very commonly used overland route, with plentiful connections by bus, minibus, share-taxi and train, most of them routed through the southern Thai city and transport hub of Hat Yai. However, because of the ongoing violence in Thailand's deep south (see Trang town), all major Western governments are currently advising people not to travel to or through Songkhla, Pattani, Yala and Narathiwat provinces, unless essential (and consequently most insurance companies are not covering travel there). This encompasses Hat Yai and the following border crossings to and from Malaysia: at Padang Besar, on the main rail line connecting Butterworth in Malaysia (and, ultimately, Kuala Lumpur and Singapore) with Hat Yai and Bangkok; at

Sungai Kolok, terminus of a railway line from Hat Yai and Bangkok, and at adjacent Ban Taba, both of which are connected by road to nearby Kota Bharu in Malaysia; and at the road crossings at Sadao, south of Hat Yai, and at Betong, south of Yala. (The routes towards Kota Bharu and Betong pass through particularly volatile territory, with martial law declared in Pattani, Yala and Narathiwat provinces; however, martial law is not in effect in Hat Yai itself.)

Nevertheless, the provinces of Trang and Satun on the west coast are not affected, and it's still perfectly possible to travel overland via Satun: by ferry between Satun's Thammalang pier and Kuala Perlis or the island of Langkawi, or overland between Ban Khuan and Kangar; or by boat between Ko Lipe and Langkawi (see Getting around). For up-to-the-minute advice, consult your government travel advisory.

Most Western tourists can spend thirty days in Malaysia and fourteen days in Singapore without having bought a visa beforehand, and there are useful Thai embassies or consulates in Kuala Lumpur, Kota Bharu, Penang and Singapore (see Border runs, extensions and re-entry permits).

Getting around

Travel in Thailand is inexpensive and efficient, if not always speedy. Unless you travel by plane, long-distance journeys in Thailand can be arduous, especially if a shoestring budget restricts you to hard seats and no air conditioning.

Nonetheless, the wide range of transport options makes travelling around Thailand easier than elsewhere in Southeast Asia. Buses are fast, cheap and frequent, and can be quite luxurious; trains are slower but safer and offer more chance of sleeping during overnight trips; moreover, if travelling by day you're likely to follow a more scenic route by rail than by road. Inter-town songthaews, air-conditioned minibuses and share-taxis are handy, and ferries provide easy access to all major islands. Local transport comes in all sorts of permutations, both public and chartered.

Inter-town buses

Buses, overall the most convenient way of getting around the country, come in four main categories. In ascending order of comfort, speed and cost, they are ordinary buses (rot thammadaa; not air-conditioned, usually orange-coloured) and three types of air-con bus (rot air or rot thua; usually blue): second-class, first-class and VIP. Ordinary and many air-con buses are run by Baw Khaw Saw (BKS), the government-controlled transport company, while privately owned, licensed air-con buses (rot ruam, usually translated as "join buses"), some of which operate from Baw Khaw Saw terminals, also ply the most popular long-distance routes. Be warned that long-distance overnight buses, on which some drivers are rumoured to take amphetamines to stay awake, seem to be involved in more than their fair share of accidents; because of this, some travellers prefer to do the overnight journeys by train and then make a shorter bus connection to their destination.

Ordinary and second-class

On most routes, including nearly all services out of Bangkok, second-class (baw sawng; look for the "2" on the side of the vehicle) air-con buses have now replaced ordinary buses as the main workhorses of the Thai bus system, though you'll still see plenty of the latter on shorter routes in more remote parts of the country. Whether air-con or not, these basic buses are incredibly inexpensive, generally run frequently during daylight hours, pack as many people in as possible and stop often, which slows them down considerably.

It's best to ask locally where to catch your bus. Failing that, designated bus stops are often marked by sala, small, open-sided wooden structures with bench seats, located at intervals along the main long-distance bus route through town or on the fringes of any decent-sized settlement, for example on the main highway that skirts the edge of town. Where there is only a bus shelter on the "wrong" side of the road, you can be sure that buses travelling in both directions will stop there for any waiting passengers; simply leave your bag on the right side of the road to alert the bus driver and wait in the shade. But if you're in the middle of nowhere with no sala in sight, any ordinary or second-class bus should stop for you if you flag it down.

First-class and VIP

Express services, with fewer stops, are mostly operated by first-class (baw neung; look for the "1" on the side of the vehicle) and VIP (usually written in English on the side) buses. These are your best option for long-distance journeys: you'll generally be allotted specific seats, there'll be a toilet, and on the longest journeys you may get blankets, snacks and nonstop DVDs. The first-class services have fewer seats than second-class and more leg room for reclining, VIP services fewer seats again. Other nomenclature for the top-of-the-range services is also used, especially by the private "join" companies: "999", "super VIP" (with even fewer seats), "Gold Class" and, confusingly, sometimes even "First

Class" (in imitation of airlines, with just eighteen huge, well-equipped seats).

On a lot of long-distance routes private "join" buses are indistinguishable from government ones and operate out of the same Baw Khaw Saw bus terminals. The major private companies, such as Nakhon Chai Air (t02 936 0009), Sombat Tour (t02 792 1444) and, operating out of Chiang Mai, Green Bus (t053 266480), have roughly similar fares, though naturally with more scope for price variation, and offer comparable facilities and standards of service. The opposite is unfortunately true of a number of the smaller, private, unlicensed companies, which have a poor reputation for service and comfort, but gear themselves towards foreign travellers with bargain fares and convenient timetables. The long-distance tour buses that run from Thanon Khao San in Banglamphu to Chiang Mai and Surat Thani are a case in point; though promised VIP buses, travellers on these routes frequently complain about shabby furnishings, ineffective air conditioning, unhelpful (even aggressive) drivers, lateness and a frightening lack of safety awareness – and there are frequent reports of theft from luggage on these routes, too, and even the spraying of "sleeping gas" so that hand luggage can be rifled without interruption. Generally it's best to travel with the government or licensed private bus companies from the main bus terminals (who have a reputation with their regular Thai customers to maintain) or to go by train instead – the extra comfort and peace of mind are well worth the extra baht.

Tickets and timetables

Tickets for all buses can be bought from the departure terminals, but for ordinary and second-class air-con buses it's normal to buy them on board. First-class and VIP buses may operate from a separate station or office, and tickets for the more popular routes should be booked a day in advance. As a rough indication of fares, a trip from Bangkok to Chiang

Mai, a distance of 700km, costs B600–800 for VIP, around B500 for first-class air-con and B400 for second-class air-con.

Long-distance buses often depart in clusters around the same time (early morning or late at night, for example), leaving a gap of five or more hours during the day with no services at all. Local TAT offices occasionally keep up-to-date bus timetables, but the best source of information, apart from the bus stations themselves, is wthaiticketmajor.com, which carries timetables in English for 360 routes as well as useful information on how to buy tickets in advance. Options include buying them online through the site; by phone on t02 262 3456 (making your payment within five hours at, for example, any branch of 7–Eleven); and buying them at 83 major post offices (as listed on the site), including the GPO in Bangkok, the Ratchadamnoen post office in Banglamphu and the Thanon Na Phra Lan post office opposite the entrance to the Grand Palace in Ratanakosin.

Songthaews, share-taxis and air-conditioned minibuses

In rural areas, the bus network is often supplemented by songthaews (literally "two rows"), which are open-ended vans (or occasionally cattle-trucks) onto which the drivers squash as many passengers as possible on two facing benches, leaving latecomers to swing off the running board at the back. As well as their essential role within towns (see Local transport), songthaews ply set routes from larger towns out to their surrounding suburbs and villages, and, where there's no call for a regular bus service, between small towns: some have destinations written on in Thai, but few are numbered. In most towns you'll find the songthaew "terminal" near the market; to pick one up between destinations just flag it down. To indicate to the driver that you want to get out, the normal practice is to rap hard with a coin on the metal railings as you approach the spot (or press the bell if there is one).

In the deep south they do things with a little more style – share-taxis connect many of the major towns, though they are inexorably being replaced by more comfortable air-conditioned minibuses (rot tuu, meaning "cupboard cars"). Scores of similar private air-conditioned minibus services are now cropping up all over the country, generally operating out of small offices or pavement desks in town centres – or from the roads around Bangkok's Victory Monument. Some of these services have a timetable, but many just aim to leave when they have a full complement of passengers; then again, some companies publish a timetable but depart when they're full – whether before or after the published time. They cover the distance faster than buses, but often at breakneck speed and they can be uncomfortably cramped when full – they're not ideal for travellers with huge rucksacks, who may be required to pay extra. These services are usually licensed and need to keep up their reputation with their regular Thai passengers but, as with full-sized buses (see Tickets and timetables), you should be wary of unlicensed private companies that offer minibuses solely for farangs from Bangkok's Thanon Khao San.

In many cases, long-distance songthaews and air-conditioned minibuses will drop you at an exact address (for example a particular guesthouse) if you warn them far enough in advance. As a rule, the cost of inter-town songthaews is comparable to that of air-con buses, that of air-conditioned minibuses perhaps a shade more.

Trains

Managed by the State Railway of Thailand (SRT), the rail network consists of four main lines and a few branch lines. The Northern Line connects Bangkok with Chiang Mai via Ayutthaya, Lopburi, Phitsanulok and Lampang. The Northeastern Line splits into two just beyond Ayutthaya, the lower branch running eastwards to Ubon Ratchathani via Khorat and Surin, the more northerly branch linking the capital with Nong Khai (with a short extension over the Mekong into Laos) via Khon Kaen and Udon Thani. The Eastern Line also has two branches, one of which runs from Bangkok to Aranyaprathet on the Cambodian border, the other of which connects Bangkok with Si Racha and Pattaya. The Southern Line extends via Hua Hin, Chumphon and Surat Thani, with spurs off to Trang and Nakhon Si Thammarat, to Hat Yai, where it branches: one line continues down the west coast of Malaysia, via Butterworth, where you usually change trains for Kuala Lumpur and Singapore; the other heads down the eastern side of the peninsula to Sungai Kolok on the Thailand–Malaysia border (20km from Pasir Mas on Malaysia's interior railway). At Nakhon Pathom a branch of this line veers off to Nam Tok via Kanchanaburi – this is all that's left of the Death Railway, of Bridge on the River Kwai notoriety.

Fares depend on the class of seat, whether or not you want air conditioning, and on the speed of the train; those quoted here exclude the "speed" supplements (see Train information and booking). Hard, wooden or thinly padded third-class seats are much cheaper than buses (Bangkok–Chiang Mai B121, or B221 with air-conditioner), and are fine for about three hours, after which numbness sets in. For longer journeys you'd be wise to opt for the padded and often reclining seats in second class (Bangkok–Chiang Mai B281, or B391 with air-conditioner). On long-distance trains, you also usually have the option of second-class berths (Bangkok–Chiang Mai B381–431, or B491–631 with air-conditioner), with day seats that convert into comfortable curtained-off bunks in the evening; lower bunks, which are more expensive than upper, have a few cubic centimetres more of space, a little more shade from the lights in the carriage, and a window. Female passengers can sometimes request a berth in an all-female section of a carriage. Travelling first class (Bangkok–Surat B1063–1263 per person) generally means a two-person air-con sleeping compartment, complete with washbasin.

There are several different types of train: slowest of all is the third-class-only Ordinary service, which is generally (but not always) available only on short and medium-length journeys and has no speed supplement. Next comes the misleadingly named Rapid train (B20–110 supplement), a trip on which from Bangkok to Chiang Mai, for example, takes fifteen hours; the Express (B150 supplement), which does the Chiang Mai route in about the same time; and the Special Express (B170–190 supplement) which covers the ground in around fourteen hours. Among the last-mentioned, fastest of all are the mostly daytime Special Express Diesel Railcars, which can usually be relied on to run roughly on time (most other services pay only lip service to their timetables). Nearly all long-distance trains have dining cars, and rail staff will also bring meals to your seat.

Booking at least one day in advance is strongly recommended for second- and first-class seats on all lengthy journeys, and sleepers should be booked as far in advance as possible (reservations open sixty days before departure). You can make bookings for any journey in Thailand at the train station in any major town, and it's now also possible to book online, at least two days in advance, at SRT's w

thairailticket.com. The website is allocated only a limited number of seats, but it allows you to pay by credit card and simply print off your ticket. Otherwise, you can arrange advance bookings over the internet with reputable Thai travel agencies such as Thai Focus (wthaifocus.com) or Thailand Train Ticket (wthailandtrainticket.com). Trains out of Bangkok can be booked in person at Hualamphong Station.

Ferries

Regular ferries connect all major islands with the mainland, and for the vast majority of crossings you simply buy your ticket on board. Safety standards are generally just about adequate but there have been a small number of sinkings in recent years – avoid travelling on boats that are clearly overloaded or in poor condition. In tourist areas competition ensures that prices are kept low, and fares tend to vary with the speed of the crossing: thus Chumphon–Ko Tao costs between B200 (6hr) and B600 (1hr 45min).

On the east coast and the Andaman coast boats generally operate a reduced service during the monsoon season (May–Oct), when the more remote spots become inaccessible. Ferries in the Samui archipelago are fairly constant year-round. Details on island connections are given in the relevant chapters.

Flights

Thai Airways (thaiairways.com) and Bangkok Airways (wbangkokair.com) are the major full-service airlines on the internal flight network, which extends to all parts of the country, using some two-dozen airports. Air Asia (wairasia.com), Nok Air (wnokair.com), which is part-owned by Thai Airways, and Orient Thai (formerly One-Two-Go; wflyorientthai.com) provide the main, "low-cost" competition; Thai Airways are also about to set up a new low-cost arm, Thai Smile. In a recently deregulated but ever-expanding market, other smaller airlines come and go with surprising frequency – and while they are operating, schedules tend to be erratic and flights are sometimes cancelled.

In some instances a flight can save you days of travelling: a flight from Chiang Mai to Phuket with Thai Airways or Air Asia, for example, takes two hours, as against a couple of days by meandering train and/or bus. Book early if possible – you can reserve online with all companies – as fares fluctuate wildly. For a fully flexible economy ticket, Bangkok to

Chiang Mai costs around B4000 with Thai Airways, but you'll find flights on the same route with the "low-cost" carriers for under B1000 (with restrictions on changes), if you book online far enough in advance.

If you're planning to make lots of domestic flights, you might want to consider the airpasses offered by Thai or Bangkok Airways – their complex conditions and prices are posted on their websites.

Local transport

Most sizeable towns have some kind of local transport system, comprising a network of buses, songthaews or even longtail boats, with set fares and routes but not rigid timetabling – in many cases vehicles wait until they're full before they leave.

Buses and songthaews

A few larger cities such as Bangkok, Khorat, Ubon Ratchathani and Phitsanulok have a local bus network that usually extends to the suburbs and operates from dawn till dusk (through the night in Bangkok). Most vehicles display route numbers in Western numerals – see the relevant accounts for further details.

Within medium-sized and large towns, the main transport role is often played by songthaews. The size and shape of vehicle used varies from town to town – and in some places they're known as "tuk-tuks" from the noise they make, not to be confused with the smaller tuk-tuks, described below, that operate as private taxis – but all have the tell-tale two facing benches in the back. In some towns, especially in the northeast, songthaews follow fixed routes; in others such as Chiang Mai, they act as communal taxis, picking up a number of people who are going in roughly the same direction and taking each of them right to their destination. To hail a songthaew just flag it down, and to indicate that you want to get out, either rap hard with a coin on the metal railings, or ring the bell if there is one. Fares within towns are around B10–20, depending on distance.

Longtail boats

Wherever there's a decent public waterway, there'll be a longtail boat ready to ferry you along it. Another great Thai trademark, these elegant, streamlined boats are powered by deafening diesel engines – sometimes custom-built, more often adapted from cars or trucks – which drive a propeller mounted on a long shaft that is swivelled for steering. Longtails carry between eight and twenty passengers: generally you'll have to charter the whole boat, but on popular fixed routes, for example between small, inshore islands and the mainland, it's cheaper to wait until the boatman gets his quorum.

Taxi services

Taxis also come in many guises, and in bigger towns you can often choose between taking a tuk-tuk, a samlor and a motorbike taxi. The one thing common to all modes of chartered transport, bar metered taxis in Bangkok and one or two cities in the northeast, is that you must establish the fare beforehand: although drivers nearly always pitch their first offers too high, they do calculate with traffic and time of day in mind, as well as according to distance – if successive drivers scoff at your price, you know you've got it wrong.

Tuk-tuks

Named after the noise of its excruciatingly unsilenced engine, the three-wheeled, open-sided tuk-tuk is the classic Thai vehicle. Painted in primary colours, tuk-tuks blast their way round towns and cities on two-stroke engines, zipping around faster than any car and taking corners on two wheels. They aren't as dangerous as they look though, and can be an exhilarating way to get around, as long as you're not too fussy about exhaust fumes. Fares come in at around B60 for a medium-length journey (over B100 in Bangkok) regardless of the number of passengers – three is the safe maximum, though six is not uncommon. It's worth paying attention to advice on how to avoid getting ripped off by Bangkok tuk-tuk drivers.

Samlors

Tuk-tuks are also sometimes known as samlors (literally "three wheels"), but the original samlors are tricycle rickshaws propelled by pedal power alone. Slower and a great deal more stately than tuk-tuks, samlors still operate in one or two towns around the country.

A further permutation are the motorized samlors (often called "skylabs" in northeastern Thailand), where the driver relies on a motorbike rather than a bicycle to propel passengers to their destination. They look much the same as cycle samlors, but often sound as noisy as tuk-tuks.

Motorbike taxis

and more precarious than tuk-tuks, motorbike taxis feature
/ns and in out-of-the-way places. In towns – where the drivers
are identified by coloured, numbered vests – they have the advantage of
being able to dodge traffic jams, but are obviously only really suitable
for the single traveller, and motorbike taxis aren't the easiest mode of
transport if you're carrying luggage. In remote spots, on the other hand,
they're often the only alternative to hitching or walking, and are
especially useful for getting between bus stops on main roads, around
car-free islands and to national parks or ancient ruins.

Within towns motorbike-taxi fares can start at B10 for very short
journeys, but for trips to the outskirts the cost rises steeply – reckon on
at least B200 for a 20km round trip.

Vehicle rental

Despite first impressions, a high accident rate and the obvious mayhem
that characterizes Bangkok's roads, driving yourself around Thailand
can be fairly straightforward. Many roads, particularly in the northeast
and the south, are remarkably uncongested. Major routes are clearly
signed in English, though this only applies to some minor roads;
unfortunately there is no perfect English-language map to compensate.

Outside the capital, the eastern seaboard and the major tourist resorts of
Ko Samui and Phuket, local drivers are generally considerate and
unaggressive; they very rarely use their horns for example, and will
often indicate and even swerve away when it's safe for you to overtake.
The most inconsiderate and dangerous road-users in Thailand are bus
drivers and lorry drivers, many of whom drive ludicrously fast, hog the
road, race round bends on the wrong side of the road and use their horns
remorselessly; worse still, many of them are tanked up on
amphetamines, which makes them quite literally fearless.

Bus and lorry drivers are at their worst after dark (many of them only
drive then), so it's best not to drive at night – a further hazard being the

inevitable stream of unlit bicycles and mopeds in and around built-up areas, as well as poorly signed roadworks, which are often not made safe or blocked off from unsuspecting traffic. Orange signs, or sometimes just a couple of tree branches or a pile of stones on the road, warn of hazards ahead.

As for local rules of the road, Thais drive on the left, and the speed limit is 60kph within built-up areas and 90kph outside them. Beyond that, there are few rules that are generally followed – you'll need to keep your concentration up and expect the unexpected from fellow road-users. Watch out especially for vehicles pulling straight out of minor roads, when you might expect them to give way. An oncoming vehicle flashing its lights means it's coming through no matter what; a right indicator signal from the car in front usually means it's not safe for you to overtake, while a left indicator signal usually means that it is safe to do so.

Theoretically, foreigners need an international driver's licence to rent any kind of vehicle, but most car-rental companies accept national licences, and the smaller operations have been known not to ask for any kind of proof whatsoever; motorbike renters very rarely bother. A popular rip-off on islands such as Ko Pha Ngan is for small agents to charge renters exorbitant amounts for any minor damage to a jeep or motorbike, even paint chips, that they find on return – they'll claim that it's very expensive to get a new part shipped over from the mainland. Be sure to check out any vehicle carefully before renting.

Petrol (nam man, which can also mean oil) currently costs around B38 a litre, gasohol, which can be used in most rental cars (though it's worth checking), B36 a litre. The big fuel stations are the least costly places to fill up (hai tem), and many of these also have toilets, mini-marts and restaurants, though some of the more decrepit-looking fuel stations on the main highways only sell diesel. Most small villages have easy-to-spot roadside huts where the fuel is pumped out of a large barrel.

Renting a car

If you decide to rent a car, go to a reputable dealer, such as Avis, Budget or National, or a rental company recommended by TAT, and make sure you get insurance from them. There are international car-rental places at many airports, including Bangkok's Suvarnabhumi, which is not a bad place to kick off, as you're on the edge of the city and within fairly easy, signposted reach of the major regional highways.

Car-rental places in provincial capitals and resorts are listed in the relevant accounts in this book. The price of a small car at a reputable company can start as low as B900 per day if booked online. In some parts of the country, including Chiang Mai, you'll still be able to rent a car or air-conditioned minibus with driver, which will cost from around B1000 for a local day-trip, more for a longer day-trip, up to about B3000 per day for a multi-day trip, including the driver's keep and petrol.

Jeeps or basic four-wheel drives are a lot more popular with farangs, especially on beach resorts and islands like Pattaya, Phuket and Ko Samui, but they're notoriously dangerous; a huge number of tourists manage to roll their jeeps on steep hillsides and sharp bends. Jeep rental usually works out somewhere around B1000–1200 per day.

International companies will accept your credit-card details as surety, but smaller agents will usually want to hold on to your passport.

Renting a motorbike

One of the best ways of exploring the countryside is to rent a motorbike, an especially popular option in the north of the country. You'll never be asked for a driving licence, but take it easy out there – Thailand's roads are not really the place to learn to ride a motorbike from scratch. Bikes of around 100cc, either fully automatic or with step-through gears, are best for inexperienced riders, but aren't really suited for long slogs. If you're going to hit the dirt roads you'll certainly need something more powerful, like a 125–250cc trail bike. These have the edge in gear choice and are the best bikes for steep slopes, though an inexperienced rider may find these machines a handful; the less widely available 125–250cc road bikes are easier to control and much cheaper on fuel.

Rental prices for the day usually work out at somewhere around B150–200 for a small bike and B500 for a good trail bike, though you can bargain for a discount on a long rental. Renters will often ask for a deposit and your passport or credit-card details; insurance is not often available, so it's a good idea to make sure your travel insurance covers you for possible mishaps.

Before signing anything, check the bike thoroughly – test the brakes, look for oil leaks, check the treads and the odometer, and make sure the chain isn't stretched too tight (a tight chain is more likely to break) – and preferably take it for a test run. As you will have to pay an inflated price for any damage when you get back, make a note on the contract of any defects such as broken mirrors, indicators and so on. Make sure you know what kind of fuel the bike takes as well.

As far as equipment goes, a helmet is essential – most rental places provide poorly made ones, but they're better than nothing. Helmets are obligatory on all motorbike journeys, and the law is often rigidly enforced with on-the-spot fines in major tourist resorts. You'll need sunglasses if your helmet doesn't have a visor. Long trousers, a long-sleeved top and decent shoes will provide a second skin if you go over, which most people do at some stage. Pillions should wear long trousers to avoid getting nasty burns from the exhaust. For the sake of stability, leave most of your luggage in baggage storage and pack as small a bag as possible, strapping it tightly to the bike with bungy cords – these can usually be provided. Once on the road, oil the chain at least every other day, keep the radiator topped up and fill up with oil every 300km or so.

For expert advice on motorbike travel in Thailand, check out David Unkovich's website (wgt-rider.com).

Cycling

The options for cycling in Thailand are numerous, whether you choose to ride the length of the country from the Malaysian border to Chiang Rai, or opt for a dirt-road adventure in the mountains around Chiang Mai. Most Thai roads are in good condition and clearly signposted; although the western and northern borders are mountainous, the rest of the country is surprisingly flat. The secondary roads (distinguished by their three-digit numbers) are paved but carry far less traffic than the main arteries and are the preferred cycling option. Traffic is reasonably well behaved and personal safety is not a major concern as long as you "ride to survive"; dogs, however, can be a nuisance on minor roads so it's probably worth having rabies shots before your trip. There are bike shops in nearly every town, and basic equipment and repairs are cheap.

Unless you head into the remotest regions around the Burmese border you are rarely more than 25km from food, water and accommodation. Overall, the best time to cycle is during the cool, dry season from November to February and the least good from April to July.

The traffic into and out of Bangkok is dense so it's worth hopping on a bus or train for the first 50–100km to your starting point. Intercity buses, taxis and most Thai domestic planes will carry your bike free of charge. Intercity trains will only transport your bike (for a cargo fare – about the price of a person) if there is a luggage carriage attached, unless you dismantle it and carry it as luggage in the compartment with you. Songthaews will carry your bike on the roof for a fare (about the price of a person).

Local one-day cycle tours and bike-rental outlets (B30–100 per day) are listed throughout this book. There are also a number of organized cycle tours, both nationwide and in northern Thailand (see Trekking and other outdoor activities in Chiang Mai). A very useful English-language resource is wbicyclethailand.com, while Biking Asia with Mr Pumpy (wmrpumpy.net) gives detailed but dated accounts of some cycling routes in Thailand.

Cycling practicalities

Strong, light, quality mountain bikes are the most versatile choice. 26-inch wheels are standard throughout Thailand and are strongly recommended; dual-use (combined road and off-road) tyres are best for touring. As regards panniers and equipment, the most important thing is to travel light. Carry a few spare spokes, but don't overdo it with too many tools and spares; parts are cheap in Thailand and most problems can be fixed quickly at any bike shop.

Bringing your bike from home is the best option as you are riding a known quantity. Importing it by plane should be straightforward, but check with the airlines for details. Most Asian airlines do not charge extra.

Buying in Thailand is also a possibility: the range is reasonable and prices tend to be cheaper than in the West or Australia. In Bangkok, the best outlet is Probike at 237/2 Thanon Rajdamri (actually off Soi Sarasin next to Lumphini Park; t02 253 3384, wprobike.co.th); Velo Thailand also sell international-brand aluminium-frame bikes, as well as renting mountain bikes for B300 per day. You can also rent good mountain bikes through the Bangkok cycle-tour operator Spice Roads (t02 712 5305, wspiceroads.com) for B280–400 per day. There are a few good outlets in Chiang Mai, too (see also wchiangmaicycling.org): Cacti, who also rent all manner of mountain and city bikes; Chaitawat, on Thanon Phra Pokklao, south off Thanon Ratchamankha, on the right (t053 279890); and Canadian-owned Top Gear, 173 Thanon Chang Moi (t053 233450).

Hitching

Public transport being so inexpensive, you should only have to resort to hitching in the most remote areas, in which case you'll probably get a lift to the nearest bus or songthaew stop quite quickly. On routes served by buses and trains, hitching is not standard practice, but in other places locals do rely on regular passers-by (such as national park officials), and you can make use of this "service" too. As with hitching anywhere in the world, think twice about hitching solo or at night, especially if you're female. Like bus drivers, truck drivers are notorious users of amphetamines, so you may want to wait for a safer offer.

Accommodation

For the simplest double room, prices start at a bargain B150 in the outlying regions, B200 in Bangkok, and B400 in the pricier resorts. Tourist centres invariably offer a tempting range of more upmarket choices but in these areas rates fluctuate according to demand, plummeting during the off-season, peaking over the Christmas fortnight and, in some places, rising at weekends throughout the year.

Bangkok and Chiang Mai are the country's big culinary centres, boasting the cream of gourmet Thai restaurants and the best international cuisines. The rest of the country is by no means a gastronomic wasteland, however, and you can eat well and cheaply in even the smallest provincial towns, many of which offer the additional attraction of regional specialities. In fact you could eat more than adequately without ever entering a restaurant, as itinerant food vendors hawking hot and cold snacks materialize in even the most remote spots, as well as on trains and buses – and night markets often serve customers from dusk until dawn.

Hygiene is a consideration when eating anywhere in Thailand, but being too cautious means you'll end up spending a lot of money and missing out on some real local treats. Wean your stomach gently by avoiding excessive amounts of chillies and too much fresh fruit in the first few days.

You can be pretty sure that any noodle stall or curry shop that's permanently packed with customers is a safe bet. Furthermore, because most Thai dishes can be cooked in under five minutes, you'll rarely have to contend with stuff that's been left to smoulder and stew. Foods that are generally considered high risk include salads, ice cream, shellfish and raw or undercooked meat, fish or eggs. If you're really concerned about health standards you could stick to restaurants and food stalls displaying a "Clean Food Good Taste" sign, part of a food sanitation project set up by the Ministry of Public Health, TAT and the Ministry of the Interior.

Most restaurants in Thailand are open every day for lunch and dinner; we've given full opening hours throughout the Guide. In a few of the country's most expensive restaurants, mostly in Bangkok, a ten percent service charge and possibly even seven percent VAT may be added to your bill.

For those interested in learning Thai cookery, short courses designed for visitors are held in Bangkok, Chiang Mai and dozens of other tourist centres around the country.

Where to eat

A lot of tourists eschew the huge range of Thai places to eat, despite their obvious attractions, and opt instead for the much "safer" restaurants in guesthouses and hotels. Almost all tourist accommodation has a kitchen, and while some are excellent, the vast majority serve up bland imitations of Western fare alongside equally pale versions of common Thai dishes. Having said that, it can be a relief to get your teeth into a processed-cheese sandwich after five days' trekking in the jungle, and guesthouses do serve comfortingly familiar Western breakfasts.

Throughout the country most inexpensive Thai restaurants and cafés specialize in one general food type or preparation method, charging around B40–50 a dish – a "noodle shop", for example, will do fried noodles and/or noodle soups, plus maybe a basic fried rice, but they won't have curries or meat or fish dishes. Similarly, a restaurant displaying whole roast chickens and ducks in its window will offer these sliced, usually with chillies and sauces and served over rice, but their menu probably won't extend to noodles or fish, while in "curry shops" your options are limited to the vats of curries stewing away in the hot cabinet.

To get a wider array of low-cost food, it's sometimes best to head for the local night market (talaat yen), a term for the gatherings of open-air night-time kitchens found in every town. Sometimes operating from 6pm to 6am, they are typically to be found on permanent patches close to the fruit and vegetable market or the bus station, and as often as not they're the best and most entertaining places to eat, not to mention the least expensive – after a lip-smacking feast of savoury dishes, a fruit drink and a dessert you'll come away no more than B150 poorer.

A typical night market has maybe thirty-odd "specialist" pushcart kitchens (rot khen) jumbled together, each fronted by several sets of tables and stools. Noodle and fried-rice vendors always feature prominently, as do sweets stalls, heaped high with sticky rice cakes wrapped in banana leaves or thick with bags of tiny sweetcorn pancakes hot from the griddle – and no night market is complete without its fruit-drink stall, offering banana shakes and freshly squeezed orange, lemon and tomato juices. In the best setups you'll find a lot more besides: curries, barbecued sweetcorn, satay sticks of pork and chicken, deep-fried insects, fresh pineapple, watermelon and mango and – if the town's by a river or near the sea – heaps of fresh fish. Having decided what you want, you order from the cook (or the cook's dogsbody) and sit down at the nearest table; there is no territorialism about night markets, so it's normal to eat several dishes from separate stalls and rely on the nearest cook to sort out the bill.

Some large markets, particularly in Bangkok, have separate food court areas where you buy coupons first and select food and drink to their value at the stalls of your choice. This is also usually the modus operandi in the food courts found in department stores and shopping centres across the country.

For a more relaxing ambience, Bangkok and the larger towns have a range of upmarket restaurants, some specializing in "royal" Thai cuisine, which is differentiated mainly by the quality of the ingredients, the complexity of preparation and the way the food is presented. Great care is taken over how individual dishes look: they are served in small portions and decorated with carved fruit and vegetables in a way that used to be the prerogative of royal cooks, but has now filtered down to the common folk. The cost of such delights is not prohibitive, either – a meal in one of these places is unlikely to cost more than B500 per person.

How to eat

Thai food is eaten with a fork (left hand) and a spoon (right hand); there is no need for a knife as food is served in bite-sized chunks, which are forked onto the spoon and fed into the mouth. Cutlery is often delivered to the table wrapped in a perplexingly tiny pink napkin: Thais use this, not for their lap, but to give their fork, spoon and plate an extra wipe-down before they eat. Steamed rice (khao) is served with most meals, and indeed the most commonly heard phrase for "to eat" is kin khao (literally, "eat rice"). Chopsticks are provided only for noodle dishes, and northeastern sticky-rice dishes are always eaten with the fingers of your right hand. Never eat with the fingers of your left hand, which is used for washing after going to the toilet.

So that complementary taste combinations can be enjoyed, the dishes in a Thai meal are served all at once, even the soup, and shared communally. The more people, the more taste and texture sensations; if there are only two of you, it's normal to order three dishes, plus your own individual plates of steamed rice, while three diners would order four dishes, and so on. Only put a serving of one dish on your rice plate each time, and then only one or two spoonfuls.

Bland food is anathema to Thais, and restaurant tables everywhere come decked out with condiment sets featuring the four basic flavours (salty, sour, sweet and spicy): usually fish sauce with chopped chillies; vinegar with chopped chillies; sugar; and dried chillies – and often extra bowls of ground peanuts and a bottle of chilli ketchup as well. Similarly, many individual Thai dishes are served with their own specific, usually spicy, condiment dip (nam jim). If you do bite into a chilli, the way to combat the searing heat is to take a mouthful of plain rice and/or beer: swigging water just exacerbates the sensation.

What to eat

Five fundamental tastes are identified in Thai cuisine – spiciness, sourness, bitterness, saltiness and sweetness – and diners aim to share a variety of dishes that impart a balance of these flavours, along with complementary textures. Lemon grass, basil, coriander, galangal, chilli, garlic, lime juice, coconut milk and fermented fish sauce are just some of the distinctive components that bring these tastes to life. A detailed food and drink glossary can be found at the end of "Contexts".

Curries and soups

Thai curries (kaeng) have a variety of curry pastes as their foundation: elaborate blends of herbs, spices, garlic, shallots and chilli peppers ground together with pestle and mortar. The use of some of these spices, as well as coconut cream, was imported from India long ago; curries that don't use coconut cream are naturally less sweet and thinner, with the consistency of soups. While some curries, such as kaeng karii (mild and yellow) and kaeng matsaman ("Muslim curry", with potatoes, peanuts and usually beef), still show their roots, others have been adapted into quintessentially Thai dishes, notably kaeng khiaw wan (sweet and green), kaeng phet (red and hot) and kaeng phanaeng (thick and savoury, with peanuts). Kaeng som generally contains fish and takes its distinctive sourness from the addition of tamarind or, in the northeast, okra leaves. Traditionally eaten during the cool season, kaeng liang uses up bland vegetables, but is made aromatic with hot peppercorns.

Eaten simultaneously with other dishes, not as a starter, Thai soups often have the tang of lemon grass, kaffir lime leaves and galangal, and are sometimes made extremely spicy with chillies. Two favourites are tom kha kai, a creamy coconut chicken soup; and tom yam kung, a hot and sour prawn soup without coconut milk. Khao tom, a starchy rice soup that's generally eaten for breakfast, meets the approval of few Westerners, except as a traditional hangover cure.

Salads

One of the lesser-known delights of Thai cuisine is the yam or salad, which imparts most of the fundamental flavours in an unusual and refreshing harmony. Yam come in many permutations – with noodles, meat, seafood or vegetables – but at the heart of every variety is a liberal squirt of lime juice and a fiery sprinkling of chillies. Salads to look out for include yam som oh (pomelo), yam hua plee (banana flowers) and yam plaa duk foo (fluffy deep-fried catfish).

Noodle and rice dishes

Sold on street stalls everywhere, noodles come in assorted varieties –
including kway tiaw (made with rice flour) and ba mii (egg noodles) –
and get boiled up as soups (nam), doused in gravy (rat na) or stir-fried
(haeng, "dry", or phat, "fried"). Most famous of all is phat thai ("Thai
fry-up"), a delicious combination of noodles (usually kway tiaw), egg,
tofu and spring onions, sprinkled with ground peanuts and lime, and

often spiked with tiny dried shrimps. Other faithful standbys include fried rice (khao phat) and cheap, one-dish meals served on a bed of steamed rice, notably khao kaeng (with curry).

Regional dishes

Many of the specialities of northern Thailand originated in Burma, including khao soi, featuring both boiled and crispy egg noodles plus beef, chicken or pork in a curried coconut soup; and kaeng hang lay, a pork curry with ginger, turmeric and tamarind. Also look out for spicy dipping sauces such as nam phrik ong, made with minced pork, roast tomatoes and lemon grass, and served with crisp cucumber slices.

The crop most suited to the infertile lands of Isaan is sticky rice (khao niaw), which replaces the standard grain as the staple for northeasterners. Served in a rattan basket, it's usually eaten with the fingers, rolled up into small balls and dipped into chilli sauces. It's perfect with such spicy local delicacies as som tam, a green-papaya salad with raw chillies, green beans, tomatoes, peanuts and dried shrimps (or fresh crab). Although you'll find basted barbecued chicken on a stick (kai yaang) all over Thailand, it originated in Isaan and is especially tasty in its home region. Raw minced pork, beef or chicken is the basis of another popular Isaan and northern dish, laap, a salad that's subtly flavoured with mint and lime. A similar northeastern salad is nam tok, featuring grilled beef or pork and roasted rice powder, which takes its name, "waterfall", from its refreshing blend of complex tastes.

Aside from putting a greater emphasis on seafood, southern Thai cuisine displays a marked Malaysian and Muslim aspect as you near the border, notably in khao mok kai, the local version of a biryani: chicken and rice cooked with turmeric and other Indian spices, and served with chicken soup. Southern markets often serve khao yam for breakfast or lunch, a delicious salad of dried cooked rice, dried shrimp and grated coconut served with a sweet sauce. You'll also find many types of roti, a flatbread sold from pushcart griddles and, in its plain form, rolled with condensed milk. Other versions include savoury mataba, with minced chicken or beef, and roti kaeng, served with curry sauce for breakfast. A huge variety of curries are also dished up in the south, many substituting shrimp paste for fish sauce. Two of the most distinctive are kaeng luang, "yellow curry", featuring fish, turmeric, pineapple, squash, beans and green papaya; and kaeng tai plaa, a powerful combination of fish stomach with potatoes, beans, pickled bamboo shoots and turmeric.

Desserts

Desserts (khanom) don't really figure on most restaurant menus, but a few places offer bowls of luk taan cheum, a jellied concoction of lotus or palm seeds floating in a syrup scented with jasmine or other aromatic flowers. Coconut milk is a feature of most other desserts, notably delicious coconut ice cream, khao niaw mamuang (sticky rice with mango), and a royal Thai cuisine special of coconut custard (sangkhayaa) cooked inside a small pumpkin, whose flesh you can also eat.

Drinks

Thais don't drink water straight from the tap, and nor should you; plastic bottles of drinking water (nam plao) are sold countrywide, in even the smallest villages, for around B10 and should be used even when brushing your teeth. Cheap restaurants and hotels generally serve free jugs of boiled water, which should be fine to drink, though they are not as foolproof as the bottles. In some large towns, notably Chiang Mai, you'll come across blue-and-white roadside machines that dispense purified water for B1 for 1–2 litres (bring your own bottle).

Night markets, guesthouses and restaurants do a good line in freshly squeezed fruit juices such as lime (nam manao) and orange (nam som), which often come with salt and sugar already added, particularly upcountry. The same places will usually do fruit shakes as well, blending bananas (nam kluay), papayas (nam malakaw), pineapples (nam sapparot) and others with liquid sugar or condensed milk (or yoghurt, to make lassi). Fresh coconut water (nam maprao) is another great thirst-quencher – you buy the whole fruit dehusked, decapitated and chilled – as is pandanus-leaf juice (bai toey); Thais are also very partial to freshly squeezed sugar-cane juice (nam awy), which is sickeningly sweet.

Bottled and canned brand-name soft drinks are sold all over the place, with a particularly wide range in the ubiquitous 7-Eleven chain stores. Glass soft-drink bottles are returnable, so some shops and drink stalls have a system of pouring the contents into a small plastic bag (fastened with an elastic band and with a straw inserted) rather than charging you the extra for taking away the bottle. The larger restaurants keep their soft drinks refrigerated, but smaller cafés and shops add ice (nam khaeng) to glasses and bags. Most ice is produced commercially under hygienic conditions, but it might become less pure in transit so be wary (ice cubes are generally a better bet than shaved ice) – and don't take ice if you have diarrhoea. For those travelling with children, or just partial themselves to dairy products, UHT-preserved milk and chilled yoghurt drinks are widely available (especially at 7-Eleven stores), as are a variety of soya drinks.

Weak Chinese tea (nam chaa) makes a refreshing alternative to water and often gets served in Chinese restaurants and roadside cafés, while posher restaurants keep stronger Chinese and Western-style teas. Instant Nescafé is usually the coffee (kaafae) offered to farangs, even if freshly ground Thai-grown coffee – notably several excellent kinds of coffee from the mountains of the north – is available. If you would like to try traditional Thai coffee, most commonly found at Chinese-style cafés in the south of the country or at outdoor markets, and prepared through filtering the grounds through a cloth, ask for kaafae thung (literally, "bag coffee"; sometimes known as kaafae boran – "traditional coffee" – or kopii), normally served very bitter with sugar as well as sweetened condensed milk alongside a glass of black or Chinese tea to wash it down with. Fresh Western-style coffee (kaafae sot) in the form of Italian espresso, cappuccino and other derivatives has recently become popular among Thais, so you'll now come across espresso machines in large towns all over the country (though some of these new coffee bars, frustratingly, don't open for breakfast, as locals tend to get their fix later in the day).

Alcoholic drinks

The two most famous local beers (bia) are Singha (ask for "bia sing") and Chang, though many travellers find Singha's weaker brew, Leo, more palatable than either. In shops you can expect to pay around B30 for a 330ml bottle of these beers, B50 for a 660ml bottle. All manner of slightly pricier foreign beers are now brewed in Thailand, including Heineken and Asahi, and in the most touristy areas you'll find expensive imported bottles from all over the world.

Wine is now found on plenty of upmarket and tourist-oriented restaurant menus, but expect to be disappointed by both quality and price, which is jacked up by heavy taxation. Thai wine is now produced at several vineyards, including at Château de Loei near Phu Reua National Park in the northeast, which produces quite tasty reds, whites including a dessert wine, a rosé and brandy (see Nam Nao National Park).

At about B80 for a hip-flask-sized 375ml bottle, the local whisky is a lot better value, and Thais think nothing of consuming a bottle a night, heavily diluted with ice and soda or Coke. The most palatable and widely available of these is Mekong, which is very pleasant once you've stopped expecting it to taste like Scotch; distilled from rice, Mekong is 35 percent proof, deep gold in colour and tastes slightly sweet. If that's not to your taste, a pricier Thai rum is also available, Sang Som, made from sugar cane, and even stronger than the whisky at forty percent proof. Check the menu carefully when ordering a bottle of Mekong from a bar in a tourist area, as they often ask up to five times more than you'd pay in a guesthouse or shop. A hugely popular way to enjoy whisky or rum at beach resorts is to pick up a bucket, containing a quarter-bottle of spirit, a mixer, Red Bull, ice and several straws, for around B200: that way you get to share with your friends and build a sandcastle afterwards.

You can buy beer and whisky in food stores, guesthouses and most restaurants; bars aren't strictly an indigenous feature as Thais traditionally don't drink out without eating, but you'll find plenty of Western-style drinking holes in Bangkok and larger centres elsewhere in the country, ranging from ultra-hip haunts in the capital to basic, open-to-the-elements "bar-beers".

Culture and etiquette

Tourist literature has marketed Thailand as the "Land of Smiles" so successfully that a lot of farangs arrive in the country expecting to be forgiven any outrageous behaviour. This is just not the case: there are some things so universally sacred in Thailand that even a hint of disrespect will cause deep offence.

The monarchy

It is both socially unacceptable and a criminal offence to make critical or defamatory remarks about the royal family. Thailand's monarchy might be a constitutional one, but almost every household displays a picture of King Bhumibol and Queen Sirikit in a prominent position, and respectful crowds mass whenever either of them makes a public appearance. The second of their four children, Crown Prince Vajiralongkorn, is the heir to the throne; his younger sister, Princess Royal Maha Chakri Sirindhorn, is often on TV and in the English-language newspapers as she is involved in many charitable projects. When addressing or speaking about royalty, Thais use a special language full of deference, called rajasap (literally "royal language").

Thailand's lese-majesty laws are among the most strictly applied in the world, increasingly invoked as the Thai establishment becomes ever more uneasy over the erosion of traditional monarchist sentiments and the rise of critical voices, particularly on the internet (though these are generally quickly censored). Accusations of lese-majesty can be levelled by and against anyone, Thai national or farang, and must be investigated by the police. As a few high-profile cases involving foreigners have demonstrated, they can be raised for seemingly minor infractions, such as defacing a poster or being less than respectful in a work of fiction. Transgressions are met with jail sentences of up to 15 years.

Aside from keeping any anti-monarchy sentiments to yourself, you should be prepared to stand when the king's anthem is played at the beginning of every cinema programme, and to stop in your tracks if the town you're in plays the national anthem over its public address system – many small towns do this twice a day at 8am and again at 6pm, as do some train stations and airports. A less obvious point: as the king's head features on all Thai currency, you should never step on a coin or banknote, which is tantamount to kicking the king in the face.

Religion

Almost equally insensitive would be to disregard certain religious precepts. Buddhism plays a fundamental role in Thai culture, and Buddhist monuments should be treated with respect – which basically means wearing long trousers or knee-length skirts, covering your arms and removing your shoes whenever you visit one.

All Buddha images are sacred, however small, tacky or ruined, and should never be used as a backdrop for a portrait photo, clambered over, placed in a position of inferiority or treated in any manner that could be construed as disrespectful. In an attempt to prevent foreigners from committing any kind of transgression the government requires a special licence for all Buddha statues exported from the country (see Customs regulations).

Monks come only just beneath the monarchy in the social hierarchy, and they too are addressed and discussed in a special language. If there's a monk around, he'll always get a seat on the bus, usually right at the back. Theoretically, monks are forbidden to have any close contact with women, which means, as a female, you mustn't sit or stand next to a monk, or even brush against his robes; if it's essential to pass him something, put the object down so that he can then pick it up – never hand it over directly. Nuns, however, get treated like ordinary women.

The body

The Western liberalism embraced by the Thai sex industry is very unrepresentative of the majority Thai attitude to the body. Clothing – or the lack of it – is what bothers Thais most about tourist behaviour. You need to dress modestly when entering temples (see City of angels), but the same also applies to other important buildings and all public places. Stuffy and sweaty as it sounds, you should keep short shorts and vests for the real tourist resorts, and be especially diligent about covering up and, for women, wearing bras in rural areas. Baring your flesh on beaches is very much a Western practice: when Thais go swimming they often do so fully clothed, and they find topless and nude bathing offensive.

According to ancient Hindu belief, the head is the most sacred part of the body and the feet are the most unclean. This belief, imported into Thailand, means that it's very rude to touch another person's head or to point your feet either at a human being or at a sacred image – when sitting on a temple floor, for example, you should tuck your legs beneath you rather than stretch them out towards the Buddha. These hierarchies also forbid people from wearing shoes (which are even more unclean than feet) inside temples and most private homes, and – by extension – Thais take offence when they see someone sitting on the "head", or prow, of a boat. Putting your feet up on a table, a chair or a pillow is also considered very uncouth, and Thais will always take their shoes off if they need to stand on a train or bus seat to get to the luggage rack, for example. On a more practical note, the left hand is used for washing after going to the toilet (see Vegetarians and vegans), so Thais never use it to put food in their mouth, pass things or shake hands – as a farang though, you'll be assumed to have different customs, so left-handers shouldn't worry unduly.

Social conventions

Thais rarely shake hands, instead using the wai to greet and say goodbye and to acknowledge respect, gratitude or apology. A prayer-like gesture made with raised hands, the wai changes according to the relative status of the two people involved: Thais can instantaneously assess which wai to use, but as a farang your safest bet is to raise your hands close to your chest, bow your head and place your fingertips just below your nose. If someone makes a wai at you, you should generally wai back, but it's safer not to initiate.

Public displays of physical affection in Thailand are more common between friends of the same sex than between lovers, whether hetero- or homosexual. Holding hands and hugging is as common among male friends as with females, so if you're caressed by a Thai acquaintance of the same sex, don't assume you're being propositioned.

Finally, there are three specifically Thai concepts you're bound to come across, which may help you comprehend a sometimes laissez-faire attitude to delayed buses and other inconveniences. The first, jai yen, translates literally as "cool heart" and is something everyone tries to maintain: most Thais hate raised voices, visible irritation and confrontations of any kind, so losing one's cool can have a much more inflammatory effect than in more combative cultures. Related to this is the oft-quoted response to a difficulty, mai pen rai – "never mind", "no problem" or "it can't be helped" – the verbal equivalent of an open-handed shoulder shrug, which has its basis in the Buddhist notion of karma (see The spread of Buddhism). And then there's sanuk, the wide-reaching philosophy of "fun", which, crass as it sounds, Thais do their best to inject into any situation, even work. Hence the crowds of inebriated Thais who congregate at waterfalls and other beauty spots on public holidays (travelling solo is definitely not sanuk), the reluctance to do almost anything without high-volume musical accompaniment, and the national waterfight which takes place during Songkhran every April on streets right across Thailand.

Thai names

Although all Thais have a first name and a family name, everyone is addressed by their first name – even when meeting strangers – prefixed by the title "Khun" (Mr/Ms); no one is ever addressed as Khun Surname, and even the phone book lists people by their given name. In Thailand you will often be addressed in an anglicized version of this convention, as "Mr Paul" or "Miss Lucy" for example. Bear in mind, though, that when a man is introduced to you as Khun Pirom, his wife will definitely not be Khun Pirom as well (that would be like calling them, for instance, "Mr and Mrs Paul"). Among friends and relatives, Phii ("older brother/sister") is often used instead of Khun when addressing older familiars (though as a tourist you're on surer ground with Khun), and Nong ("younger brother/sister") is used for younger ones.

Many Thai first names come from ancient Sanskrit and have an auspicious meaning; for example, Boon means good deeds, Porn means blessings, Siri means glory and Thawee means to increase. However, Thais of all ages are commonly known by the nickname given them soon after birth rather than by their official first name. This tradition arises out of a deep-rooted superstition that once a child has been officially named the spirits will begin to take an unhealthy interest in them, so a nickname is used instead to confuse the spirits. Common nicknames – which often bear no resemblance to the adult's personality or physique – include Yai (Big), Oun (Fat) and Muu (Pig); Lek or Noi (Little), Nok (Bird), Noo (Mouse) and Kung (Shrimp); and English nicknames like Apple, Joy or even Pepsi.

Family names were only introduced in 1913 (by Rama Vl, who invented many of the aristocracy's surnames himself), and are used only in very formal situations, always in conjunction with the first name. It's quite usual for good friends never to know each other's surname. Ethnic Thais generally have short surnames like Somboon or Srisai, while the long, convoluted family names – such as Sonthanasumpun – usually indicate Chinese origin, not because they are phonetically Chinese but because many Chinese immigrants have chosen to adopt new Thai surnames and Thai law states that every newly created surname must be unique. Thus anyone who wants to change their surname must submit a shortlist of five unique Thai names – each to a maximum length of ten Thai characters – to be checked against a database of existing names. As more and more names are taken, Chinese family names get increasingly unwieldy, and more easily distinguishable from the pithy old Thai names.

The media

To keep you abreast of world affairs, there are several English-language newspapers in Thailand, though relatively mild forms of censorship (and self-censorship) affect all newspapers and the predominantly state-controlled media.

Newspapers and magazines

Of the hundreds of Thai-language newspapers and magazines published every week, the sensationalist daily tabloid Thai Rath attracts the widest readership, with circulation of around a million, while the moderately progressive Matichon is the leading quality daily, with an estimated circulation of 600,000.

Alongside these, two daily English-language papers – the Bangkok Post (wbangkokpost.com) and the Nation (wnationmultimedia.com) – are capable of adopting a fairly critical attitude to political goings-on and cover major domestic and international stories as well as tourist-related issues. The Nation, however, has recently adopted a split personality (and a more overt anti-red shirt stance) and now covers mostly business news. The Post's Spectrum supplement, which comes inside the Sunday edition, carries investigative journalism. Both the Post and Nation are sold at most newsstands in the capital as well as in major provincial towns and tourist resorts; the more isolated places receive their few copies one day late. Details of local English-language publications are given in the relevant Guide accounts.

You can also pick up foreign magazines such as Newsweek and Time in Bangkok, Chiang Mai and the major resorts. English-language bookshops such as Bookazine and some expensive hotels carry air-freighted, or sometimes locally printed and stapled, copies of foreign national newspapers for at least B50 a copy; the latter are also sold in tourist-oriented minimarkets in the big resorts.

Television

There are six government-controlled, terrestrial TV channels in Thailand: channels 3, 5 (owned and operated by the army), 7 and 9 transmit a blend of news, documentaries, soaps, sports, talk and quiz shows, while the more serious-minded PBS (formerly Thaksin Shinawatra's ITV) and NBT are public-service channels, owned and operated by the government's public relations department. Cable networks – available in many mid-range and most upmarket hotel rooms – carry channels from all around the world, including CNN from the US, BBC World from the UK and sometimes ABC from Australia, as well as English-language movie channels, MTV and various sports and documentary channels. Both the Bangkok Post and the Nation print the daily TV and cable schedule.

Radio

Thailand boasts over five hundred radio stations, mostly music-oriented, ranging from Virgin Radio's Eazy (105.5 FM), which serves up Western pop, through luk thung on 95FM, to Fat Radio, which plays Thai indie sounds (104.5 FM). Chulalongkorn University Radio (101.5 FM) plays classical music from 9.30pm to midnight every night. Net 107 on 107 FM is one of several stations that include English-language news bulletins.

With a shortwave radio – or by going online – you can pick up the BBC World Service (wbbc.co.uk/worldservice), Radio Australia (wradioaustralia.net.au), Voice of America (wvoanews.com), Radio Canada (wrcinet.ca) and other international stations right across Thailand. Times and wavelengths change regularly, so get hold of a recent schedule just before you travel or consult the websites for frequency and programme guides.

Festivals

Nearly all Thai festivals have a religious aspect. The most theatrical are generally Brahmin (Hindu) in origin, honouring elemental spirits and deities with ancient rites and ceremonial costumed parades. Buddhist celebrations usually revolve round the local temple, and while merit-making is a significant feature, a light-hearted atmosphere prevails, as the wat grounds are swamped with food and trinket vendors and makeshift stages are set up to show likay folk theatre, singing stars and beauty contests.

Many of the secular festivals (like the elephant roundups and the Bridge over the River Kwai spectacle) are outdoor local culture shows, geared specifically towards Thai and farang tourists. Others are thinly veiled but lively trade fairs held in provincial capitals to show off the local speciality, be it exquisite silk weaving or especially tasty rambutans.

Few of the dates for religious festivals are fixed, so check with TAT for specifics (wtourismthailand.org). The names of the most touristy celebrations are given here in English; the more low-key festivals are more usually known by their Thai name (ngan means "festival"). Some of the festivals below are designated as national holidays.

A festival calendar

January–March

Chinese New Year Nakhon Sawan (three days between mid-Jan and late Feb). In Nakhon Sawan, the new Chinese year is welcomed in with particularly exuberant parades of dragons and lion dancers, Chinese opera performances, an international lion-dance competition and a fireworks display. Also celebrated in Chinatowns across the country, especially in Bangkok and Phuket.

Flower Festival Chiang Mai (usually first weekend in Feb). Enormous floral sculptures are paraded through the streets.

Makha Puja Nationwide (particularly Wat Benjamabophit in Bangkok, Wat Phra That Doi Suthep in Chiang Mai and Wat Mahathat in Nakhon Si Thammarat; Feb full-moon day). A day of merit-making marks the occasion when 1250 disciples gathered spontaneously to hear the Buddha preach, and culminates with a candlelit procession round the local temple's bot.

Ngan Phrabat Phra Phutthabat, near Lopburi (early Feb and early March). Pilgrimages to the Holy Footprint attract food and handicraft vendors and travelling players. For more information, see Ban Vichayen.

King Narai Reign Fair Lopburi (Feb). Costumed processions and a son et lumière show at Narai's palace.

Ngan Phra That Phanom That Phanom (Feb). Thousands come to pay homage at the holiest shrine in Isaan, which houses relics of the Buddha.

Kite fights and flying contests Nationwide (particularly Sanam Luang, Bangkok; late Feb to mid-April).

April and May

Poy Sang Long Mae Hong Son and Chiang Mai (early April). Young Thai Yai boys precede their ordination into monkhood by parading the streets in floral headdresses and festive garb.

Songkhran Nationwide (particularly Chiang Mai, and Bangkok's Thanon Khao San; usually April 13–15). The most exuberant of the national festivals welcomes the Thai New Year with massive waterfights, sandcastle building in temple compounds and the inevitable parades and "Miss Songkhran" beauty contests. For more information, see Chiang Mai festivals.

Ngan Phanom Rung Prasat Hin Khao Phanom Rung (usually April). The three-day period when the sunrise is perfectly aligned through fifteen doorways at these magnificent eleventh-century Khmer ruins is celebrated with daytime processions and nightly son et lumière.

Visakha Puja Nationwide (particularly Bangkok's Wat Benjamabophit, Wat Phra That Doi Suthep in Chiang Mai and Nakhon Si Thammarat's Wat Mahathat; May full-moon day). The holiest day of the Buddhist year, commemorating the birth, enlightenment and death of the Buddha all in one go; the most public and photogenic part is the candlelit evening procession around the wat.

Raek Na Sanam Luang, Bangkok (early May). The royal ploughing ceremony to mark the beginning of the rice-planting season; ceremonially clad Brahmin leaders parade sacred oxen and the royal plough, and interpret omens to forecast the year's rice yield.

Rocket Festival Yasothon (Bun Bang Fai; weekend in mid-May). Beautifully crafted, painted wooden rockets are paraded and fired to ensure plentiful rains; celebrated all over Isaan, but especially lively in Yasothon.

June–September

Phi Ta Khon Dan Sai, near Loei (end June or beginning July). Masked re-enactment of the Buddha's penultimate incarnation.

Candle Festival Ubon Ratchathani (Asanha Puja; July, three days around the full moon). This nationwide festival marking the Buddha's first sermon and the subsequent beginning of the annual Buddhist retreat period (Khao Pansa) is celebrated across the northeast with parades of enormous wax sculptures, most spectacularly in Ubon Ratchathani.

Tamboon Deuan Sip Nakhon Si Thammarat (Sept or Oct). Merit-making ceremonies to honour dead relatives accompanied by a ten-day fair.

October–December

Vegetarian Festival Phuket and Trang (Ngan Kin Jeh; Oct or Nov). Chinese devotees become vegetarian for a nine-day period and then parade through town performing acts of self-mortification such as pushing skewers through their cheeks. Celebrated in Bangkok's Chinatown by most food vendors and restaurants turning vegetarian for about a fortnight.

Bang Fai Phaya Nak Nong Khai and around (usually Oct). The strange appearance of pink balls of fire above the Mekong River draws sightseers from all over Thailand.

Tak Bat Devo and Awk Pansa Nationwide (especially Ubon Ratchathani and Nakhon Phanom; Oct full-moon day). Offerings to monks and general merrymaking to celebrate the Buddha's descent to earth from Tavatimsa heaven and the end of the Khao Pansa retreat. Celebrated in Ubon with a procession of illuminated boats along the rivers, and in Nakhon Phanom with another illuminated boat procession and Thailand–Laos dragon-boat races along the Mekong.

Chak Phra Surat Thani (mid-Oct). The town's chief Buddha images are paraded on floats down the streets and on barges along the river.

Boat Races Nan, Nong Khai, Phimai and elsewhere (Oct to mid-Nov). Longboat races and barge parades along town rivers.

Thawt Kathin Nationwide (the month between Awk Pansa and Loy Krathong, generally Oct–Nov). During the month following the end of the monks' rainy-season retreat, it's traditional for the laity to donate new robes to the monkhood and this is celebrated in most towns with parades and a festival, and occasionally, when it coincides with a kingly anniversary, with a spectacular Royal Barge Procession down the Chao Phraya River in Bangkok.

Loy Krathong Nationwide (particularly Sukhothai and Chiang Mai; full moon in Nov). Baskets (krathong) of flowers and lighted candles are floated on any available body of water (such as ponds, rivers, lakes, canals and seashores) to honour water spirits and celebrate the end of the rainy season. Nearly every town puts on a big show, with bazaars, public entertainments, fireworks, and in Chiang Mai, the release of paper hot-air balloons; in Sukhothai it is the climax of a son et lumière festival that's held over several nights.

Ngan Wat Saket Wat Saket, Bangkok (first week of Nov). Probably Thailand's biggest temple fair, held around the Golden Mount, with all the usual festival trappings.

Elephant Roundup Surin (third weekend of Nov). Two hundred elephants play team games, perform complex tasks and parade in battle dress.

River Kwai Bridge Festival Kanchanaburi (ten nights from the last week of Nov into the first week of Dec). Spectacular son et lumière at the infamous bridge.

Silk and Phuk Siao Festival Khon Kaen (Nov 29–Dec 10). Weavers from around the province come to town to sell their lengths of silk.

World Heritage Site Festival Ayutthaya (mid-Dec). Week-long celebration, including a nightly historical son et lumière romp, to commemorate the town's UNESCO designation.

New Year's Eve Countdown Nationwide (Dec 31). Most cities and tourist destinations welcome in the new year with fireworks, often backed up by food festivals, beauty contests and outdoor performances.

Entertainment and sport

Bangkok is the best place to catch authentic performances of classical Thai dance, though more easily digestible tourist-oriented shows are staged in some of the big tourist centres as well as in Bangkok. The country's two main Thai boxing stadia are also in the capital, but you'll come across local matches in the provinces too.

Drama and dance

Drama pretty much equals dance in classical Thai theatre, and many of the traditional dance-dramas are based on the Ramakien, the Thai version of the Hindu epic the Ramayana, an adventure tale of good versus evil that is taught in all schools. Not understanding the plots can be a major disadvantage, so try reading an abridged version beforehand (see M.L. Manich Jumsai and The Ramayana/Ramakien) and check out the wonderfully imaginative murals at Wat Phra Kaeo in Bangkok. There are three broad categories of traditional Thai dance-drama – khon, lakhon and likay – described below in descending order of refinement.

Khon

The most spectacular form of traditional Thai theatre is khon, a stylized drama performed in masks and elaborate costumes by a troupe of highly trained classical dancers. There's little room for individual interpretation in these dances, as all the movements follow a strict choreography that's been passed down through generations: each graceful, angular gesture depicts a precise event, action or emotion which will be familiar to educated khon audiences. The dancers don't speak, and the story is chanted and sung by a chorus who stand at the side of the stage, accompanied by a classical phipat orchestra.

A typical khon performance features several of the best-known Ramakien episodes, in which the main characters are recognized by their masks, headdresses and heavily brocaded costumes. Gods and humans don't wear masks, but the hero Rama and heroine Sita always wear tall gilded headdresses and often appear as a trio with Rama's brother Lakshaman. Monkey masks are wide-mouthed: monkey army chief Hanuman always wears white, and his two right-hand men – Nilanol, the god of fire, and Nilapat, the god of death – wear red and black respectively. In contrast, the demons have grim mouths, clamped shut or snarling; Totsagan, king of the demons, wears a green face in battle and a gold one during peace, but always sports a two-tier headdress carved with two rows of faces.

Khon is performed with English subtitles at Bangkok's Sala Chalermkrung and is also featured within the various cultural shows staged by tourist restaurants in Bangkok, Phuket and Pattaya. Even if you don't see a show, you're bound to come across finely crafted real and replica khon masks both in museums and in souvenir shops all over the country.

Lakhon

Serious and refined, lakhon is derived from khon but is used to dramatize a greater range of stories, including Buddhist Jataka tales, local folk dramas and of course the Ramakien.

The form you're most likely to come across is lakhon chatri, which is performed at shrines like Bangkok's Erawan and at a city's lak muang as entertainment for the spirits and a token of gratitude from worshippers. Usually female, the lakhon chatri dancers perform as an ensemble, executing sequences that, like khon movements, all have minute and particular symbolism. They also wear ornate costumes, but no masks, and dance to the music of a phipat orchestra. Unfortunately, as resident shrine troupes tend to repeat the same dances a dozen times a day, it's rarely the sublime display it's cracked up to be. Bangkok's National Theatre stages the more elegantly executed lakhon nai, a dance form that used to be performed at the Thai court and often re-tells the Ramakien.

Likay

Likay is a much more popular and dynamic derivative of khon – more light-hearted, with lots of comic interludes, bawdy jokes and panto-style over-the-top acting and singing. Some likay troupes perform Ramakien excerpts, but a lot of them adapt pot-boiler romances or write their own and most will ham things up with improvisations and up-to-the-minute topical satire. Costumes might be traditional as in khon and lakhon, modern and Western as in films, or a mixture of both.

Likay troupes travel around the country doing shows on makeshift outdoor stages wherever they think they'll get an audience, most commonly at temple fairs. Performances are often free and generally last for about five hours, with the audience strolling in and out of the show, cheering and joking with the cast throughout. Televised likay dramas get huge audiences and always follow romantic soap-opera-style plot-lines. Short likay dramas are also a staple of Bangkok's National Theatre, but for more radical and internationally minded likay, look out for performances by Makhampom (wmakhampom.net), a famous, long-established troupe with bases in Bangkok and Chiang Dao that pushes likay in new directions to promote social causes and involve minority communities.

Nang

Nang, or shadow plays, are said to have been the earliest dramas performed in Thailand, but now are rarely seen except in the far south, where the Malaysian influence ensures an appreciative audience for nang thalung. Crafted from buffalo hide, the two-dimensional nang thalung puppets play out scenes from popular dramas against a backlit screen, while the storyline is told through songs, chants and musical interludes. An even rarer nang form is the nang yai, which uses enormous cut-outs of whole scenes rather than just individual characters, so the play becomes something like an animated film.

Film

All sizeable towns have a cinema or two – Bangkok has over fifty – and tickets generally start at around B80. The website wmovieseer.com lists the weekly schedule for many cinemas around the country. In some rural areas, villagers still have to make do with the travelling cinema, or nang klarng plaeng, which sets up a mobile screen in wat compounds or other public spaces, and often entertains the whole village in one sitting. However makeshift the cinema, the king's anthem is always played before every screening, during which the audience is expected to stand up.

Fast-paced Chinese blockbusters have long dominated the programmes at Thai cinemas, serving up a low-grade cocktail of sex, spooks, violence and comedy. Not understanding the dialogue is rarely a drawback, as the storylines tend to be simple and the visuals more entertaining than the words. In the cities, Western films are also popular, and new releases often get subtitled rather than dubbed. They are also quickly available as pirated DVDs sold at street stalls in the main cities and resorts.

In recent years Thailand's own film industry has been enjoying a boom, and in the larger cities and resorts you may be lucky enough to come across one of the bigger Thai hits showing with English subtitles.

Thai boxing

Thai boxing (muay thai) enjoys a following similar to football or baseball in the West: every province has a stadium and whenever the sport is shown on TV you can be sure that large noisy crowds will gather round the sets in streetside restaurants. The best place to see Thai boxing is at one of Bangkok's two main stadia, which between them hold bouts every night of the week (see Cinemas), but many tourist resorts also stage regular matches.

There's a strong spiritual and ritualistic dimension to muay thai, adding grace to an otherwise brutal sport. Each boxer enters the ring to the wailing music of a three-piece phipat orchestra, wearing the statutory red or blue shorts and, on his head, a sacred rope headband or mongkhon. Tied around his biceps are phra jiat, pieces of cloth that are often decorated with cabalistic symbols and may contain Buddhist tablets. The fighter then bows, first in the direction of his birthplace and then to the north, south, east and west, honouring both his teachers and the spirit of the ring. Next he performs a slow dance, claiming the audience's attention and demonstrating his prowess as a performer.

Any part of the body except the head may be used as an offensive weapon in muay thai, and all parts except the groin are fair targets. Kicks to the head are the blows that cause most knockouts. As the action hots up, so the orchestra speeds up its tempo and the betting in the audience becomes more frenetic. It can be a gruesome business, but it was far bloodier before modern boxing gloves were made compulsory in the 1930s, when the Queensbury Rules were adapted for muay – combatants used to wrap their fists with hemp impregnated with a face-lacerating dosage of ground glass.

A number of muay thai gyms and camps offer training courses for foreigners, including several in Bangkok, as well as Chiang Mai, Hua Hin, Ko Pha Ngan and Ko Yao Noi – see the relevant accounts for details.

Takraw

Whether in Bangkok or upcountry, you're quite likely to come across some form of takraw game being played in a public park, a school, a wat compound or just in a backstreet alley. Played with a very light rattan ball (or one made of plastic to look like rattan), the basic aim of the game is to keep the ball off the ground. To do this you can use any part of your body except your hands, so a well-played takraw game looks extremely balletic, with players leaping and arching to get a good strike.

There are at least five versions of competitive takraw, based on the same principles. The version featured in the Southeast Asian Games and most frequently in school tournaments is played over a volleyball net and involves two teams of three; the other most popular competitive version has a team ranged round a basketball-type hoop trying to score as many goals as possible within a limited time period before the next team replaces them and tries to outscore them.

Other takraw games introduce more complex rules (like kicking the ball backwards with your heels through a ring made with your arms behind your back) and many assign points according to the skill displayed by individual players rather than per goal or dropped ball.

Spas and traditional massage

With their focus on indulgent self-pampering, spas are usually associated with high-spending tourists, but the treatments on offer at Thailand's five-star hotels are often little different from those used by traditional medical practitioners, who have long held that massage and herbs are the best way to restore physical and mental well-being.

Thai massage (nuad boran) is based on the principle that many physical and emotional problems are caused by the blocking of vital energy channels within the body. The masseur uses his or her feet, heels, knees and elbows, as well as hands, to exert pressure on these channels, supplementing this acupressure-style technique by pulling and pushing the limbs into yogic stretches. This distinguishes Thai massage from most other massage styles, which are more concerned with tissue manipulation. One is supposed to emerge from a Thai massage feeling both relaxed and energized, and it is said that regular massages produce long-term benefits in muscles as well as stimulating the circulation and aiding natural detoxification.

Thais will visit a masseur for many conditions, including fevers, colds and muscle strain, but bodies that are not sick are also considered to benefit from the restorative powers of a massage, and nearly every hotel and guesthouse will be able to put you in touch with a masseur. On the more popular beaches, it can be hard to walk a few hundred metres without being offered a massage – something Thai tourists are just as enthusiastic about as foreigners. Thai masseurs do not traditionally use oils or lotions and the client is treated on a mat or mattress; you'll often be given a pair of loose-fitting trousers and perhaps a loose top to change into. English-speaking masseurs will often ask if there are any areas of your body that you would like them to concentrate on, or if you have any problem areas that you want them to avoid; if your masseur doesn't speak English, the simplest way to signal the latter is to point at the offending area while saying mai sabai ("not well"). If you're in pain during a massage, wincing usually does the trick, perhaps adding jep ("it hurts"); if your masseur is pressing too hard for your liking, say bao bao na khrap/kha ("gently please").

The best places for a basic massage are usually the government-accredited clinics and hospitals that are found in large towns all over the country. A session should ideally last at least one and a half hours and will cost from around B250. If you're a bit wary of submitting to the full works, try a foot massage first, which will apply the same techniques of acupressure and stretching to just your feet and lower legs. Most places also offer herbal massages, in which the masseur will knead you with a ball of herbs (phrakop) wrapped in a cloth and steam-heated; they're said to be particularly good for stiffness of the neck, shoulders and back.

The science behind Thai massage has its roots in Indian Ayurvedic medicine, which classifies each component of the body according to one of the four elements (earth, water, fire and air), and holds that balancing these elements within the body is crucial to good health. Many of the stretches and manipulations fundamental to Thai massage are thought to have derived from yogic practices introduced to Thailand from India by Buddhist missionaries in about the second century BC; Chinese acupuncture and reflexology have also had a strong influence. In the nineteenth century, King Rama III ordered a series of murals illustrating the principles of Thai massage to be painted around the courtyard of Bangkok's Wat Pho, and they are still in place today, along with statues of ascetics depicted in typical massage poses.

Wat Pho has been the leading school of Thai massage for hundreds of years, and it is possible to take courses there as well as to receive a massage; it also runs a residential massage school and clinic in Nakhon Pathom province (wwatpomassage.com). Masseurs who trained at Wat Pho are considered to be the best in the country and masseurs all across

Thailand advertise this as a credential, whether or not it is true. Many Thais consider blind masseurs to be especially sensitive practitioners.

While Wat Pho is the most famous place to take a course in Thai massage, many foreigners interested in learning this ancient science head for Chiang Mai, which offers the biggest concentration of massage schools (including another satellite branch of the Wat Pho school), though you will find others all over Thailand, including in Bangkok and at southern beach resorts.

All spas in Thailand feature traditional Thai massage and herbal therapies in their programmes, but most also offer dozens of other international treatments, including facials, aromatherapy, Swedish massage and various body wraps. Spa centres in upmarket hotels and resorts are usually open to non-guests but generally need to be booked in advance. Day-spas that are not attached to hotels are generally cheaper and are found in some of the bigger cities and resorts – some of these may not require reservations.

Meditation centres and retreats

Of the hundreds of meditation temples in Thailand, a few cater specifically for foreigners by holding meditation sessions and retreats in English. Novices as well as practised meditators are generally welcome at these wats, but absolute beginners might like to consider the regular retreats at Wat Suan Mokkh and Wat Khao Tham, which are conducted by supportive and experienced Thai and Western teachers and include talks and interviews on Buddhist teachings and practice. The meditation taught is mostly Vipassana, or "insight", which emphasizes the minute observation of internal sensations; the other main technique you'll come across is Samatha, which aims to calm the mind and develop concentration (these two techniques are not entirely separate, since you cannot have insight without some degree of concentration).

Longer retreats are for the serious-minded only. All the temples listed below welcome both male and female English-speakers, but strict segregation of the sexes is enforced and many places observe a vow of silence. Reading and writing are also discouraged, and you'll generally not be allowed to leave the retreat complex unless absolutely necessary, so try to bring whatever you'll need in with you. All retreats expect you to wear modest clothing, and some require you to wear white – check ahead whether there is a shop at the retreat complex or whether you are expected to bring this with you.

An average day at any one of these monasteries starts with a wake-up call at around 4am and includes several hours of group meditation and chanting, as well as time put aside for chores and personal reflection. However long their stay, visitors are usually expected to keep the eight main Buddhist precepts, the most restrictive of these being the abstention from food after midday and from alcohol, tobacco, drugs and sex at all times. Most wats ask for a minimal daily donation (around B200) to cover the costs of the simple accommodation and food.

Further details about many of the temples listed below – including how to get there – are given in the relevant sections in the Guide chapters. A useful resource is wdhammathai.org, which provides lots of general background, practical advice and details of meditation temples and centres around Thailand. In addition, wwanderingdhamma.org is a very interesting blog written by an American Ph.D. student, with some fascinating articles, information on English-speaking retreats in Thailand and lots of good links. Meanwhile, Little Bangkok Sangha (wlittlebang.org) is a handy blog maintained by a British-born monk, Phra Pandit, which gives details of talks in Bangkok and retreats. Also in Bangkok, keep an eye out for developments at the Buddhadasa Indapanno Archives in Chatuchak Park in the north of the city, a recently built centre in honour of the founder of Wat Suan Mokkh, which may well host more events for English-speakers in the future.

Meditation centres and retreat temples

House of Dhamma Insight Meditation Centre 26/9 Soi Lardprao 15, Chatuchak, Bangkok t02 511 0439, whouseofdhamma.com. Regular two-day courses in Vipassana, as well as day workshops in Metta (Loving Kindness) meditation. Courses in reiki and other subjects available.

Thailand Vipassana Centres wdhamma.org. Frequent courses in a Burmese Vipassana tradition for beginners (10 days) and practised meditators (1–45 days), in Khon Kaen, Lamphun, Phitsanulok, Prachinburi (near Bangkok) and Sangkhlaburi. Foreign students must pre-register by email (application form available on the website).

Wat Pah Nanachat Ban Bung Wai, Amphoe Warinchamrab, Ubon Ratchathani 34310 wwatpahnanachat.org. The famous monk, Ajahn Chah, established this forest monastery, 17km west of Ubon

Ratchathani, in 1975 specifically to provide monastic training for non-Thais, with English the primary language. Visitors who want to practise with the resident community are welcome, but the atmosphere is serious and intense and not for beginners or curious sightseers, and accommodation for students is limited, so you should write to the monastery before visiting, allowing several weeks to receive a written response.

Wat Phra Si Chom Thong Insight Meditation Centre t053 826869, ewatchomtong@sirimangalo.org. Located in Chom Thong, 58km south of Chiang Mai, this is the centre of the Northern Insight Meditation School developed by the well-known Phra Ajarn Tong Sirimangalo (the meditation teachers at Chiang Mai's Wat Ram Poeng and Wat Doi Suthep are all students of Phra Tong). Offers 4- to 21-day Vipassana meditation courses taught in English and Thai and some European languages as well. By donation.

World Fellowship of Buddhists (WFB) 616 Benjasiri Park, Soi Medhinivet off Soi 24, Thanon Sukhumvit, Bangkok t02 661 1284–7, wwfbhq.org. Headquarters of an influential worldwide organization of (mostly Theravada) Buddhists, founded in Sri Lanka in 1950, this is the main information centre for advice on English-speaking retreats in Thailand.

Outdoor activities

Many travellers' itineraries take in a few days' trekking in the hills and a stint snorkelling or diving off the beaches of the south. Trekking is concentrated in the north, but there are smaller, less touristy trekking operations in Kanchanaburi, Sangkhlaburi and Umphang. There are also plenty of national parks to explore and opportunities for rock climbing and kayaking.

Diving and snorkelling

Clear, warm waters (averaging 28°C), prolific marine life and affordable prices make Thailand a very rewarding place for diving and snorkelling. Most islands and beach resorts have at least one dive centre that organizes trips to outlying islands, teaches novice divers and rents out equipment, and in the bigger resorts there are dozens to choose from.

Thailand's three coasts are subject to different monsoon seasons, so you can dive all year round; the seasons run from November to April along the Andaman coast (though there is sometimes good diving here up until late Aug), and all year round on the Gulf and east coasts. Though every diver has their favourite reef, Thailand's premier diving destinations are generally considered to be Ko Similan, Ko Surin, Richelieu Rock and Hin Muang and Hin Daeng – all of them off the Andaman coast. As an accessible base for diving, Ko Tao off the Gulf coast is hard to beat, with deep, clear inshore water and a wide variety of dive sites in very close proximity.

Whether you're snorkelling or diving, try to minimize your impact on the fragile reef structures by not touching the reefs and by asking your boatman not to anchor in the middle of one; don't buy coral souvenirs, as tourist demand only encourages local entrepreneurs to dynamite reefs.

Should you scrape your skin on coral, wash the wound thoroughly with boiled water, apply antiseptic and keep protected until healed. Wearing a T-shirt is a good idea when snorkelling to stop your back from getting sunburnt.

Diving

It's usually worth having a look at several dive centres before committing yourself to a trip or a course. Always verify the dive instructors' PADI (Professional Association of Diving Instructors) or equivalent accreditation and check to see if the dive shop is a member of PADI's International Resorts and Retailers Association (IRRA) as this guarantees a certain level of professionalism. You can view a list of IRRAs in Thailand at wpadi.com.

I've highlighted IRRA dive shops that are accredited Five-Star centres, as these are considered by Padi to offer very high standards, but you should always consult other divers first if possible. Some dive operators do fake their PADI credentials. Avoid booking ahead over the internet without knowing anything else about the dive centre, and be wary of any operation offering extremely cheap courses: maintaining diving equipment is an expensive business in Thailand so any place offering unusually good rates will probably be cutting corners and compromising your safety. Ask to meet your instructor or dive leader, find out how many people there'll be in your group, check out the kind of instruction given (some courses are over-reliant on videos) and look over the equipment, checking the quality of the air in the tanks yourself and also ensuring there's an oxygen cylinder on board. Most divers prefer to travel to the dive site in a decent-sized boat equipped with a radio and emergency medical equipment rather than in a longtail. If this concerns you, ask the dive company about their boat before you sign up; firms that use longtails generally charge less.

Insurance should be included in the price of courses and introductory dives; for qualified divers, you're better off checking that your general travel insurance covers diving, though some diving shops can organize cover for you. There are recompression chambers in Pattaya, on Ko Samui and on Phuket and it's a good idea to check whether your dive centre is a member of one of these outfits, as recompression services are extremely expensive for anyone who's not.

There are a number of useful books available on diving in Thailand

Trips and courses

All dive centres run programmes of one-day dive trips (featuring two dives) and night dives for B1500–4500 (with reductions if you bring your own gear), and many of the Andaman-coast dive centres also do three- to seven-day live-aboards to the exceptional reefs off the remote Similan and Surin islands (from B11,900). Most dive centres can rent underwater cameras for about B1500 per day.

All dive centres offer a range of courses from beginner to advanced level, with equipment rental usually included in the cost; Ko Tao is now the largest, and most competitive, dive-training centre in Southeast Asia, with around fifty dive companies including plenty of PADI Five-Star centres. The most popular courses are the one-day introductory or resort dive (a pep talk and escorted shallow dive, open to anyone aged 10 or over), which costs anything from B2000 for a very local dive to B7000 for an all-inclusive day-trip to the Similan Islands; and the four-day open-water course, which entitles you to dive without an instructor (from B9800 on Ko Tao in high season). Kids' Bubblemaker courses, for children aged 8–9, cost around B2000.

Snorkelling

Boatmen and tour agents on most beaches offer snorkelling trips to nearby reefs and many dive operators welcome snorkellers to tag along for discounts of thirty percent or more; not all diving destinations are rewarding for snorkellers though, so check the relevant account in this book first. As far as snorkelling equipment goes, the most important thing is that you buy or rent a mask that fits. To check the fit, hold the mask against your face, then breathe in and remove your hands – if it falls off, it'll leak water. If you're buying equipment, you should be able to kit yourself out with a mask, snorkel and fins for about B1000, available from most dive centres. Few places rent fins, but a mask and snorkel set usually costs about B150 a day to rent, and if you're going on a snorkelling day-trip they are often included in the price.

National parks and wildlife observation

Thailand's hundred-plus national parks, which are administered by the National Park, Wildlife and Plant Conservation Department (wdnp.go.th), are generally the best places to observe wildlife. Though you're highly unlikely to encounter tigers or sun bears, you have a good chance of spotting gibbons, civets, mouse deer and hornbills and may even get to see a wild elephant. A number of wetlands also host a rewarding variety of birdlife. All parks charge an entrance fee, which for foreigners is usually B200 (B100 for children), though some charge B100 and a few charge B400.

Waymarked hiking trails in most parks are generally limited and rarely very challenging and decent park maps are hard to come by, so for serious national-park treks you'll need to hire a guide and venture beyond the public routes. Nearly all parks provide accommodation and/or campsites (see Tourist hotels). Some national parks close for several weeks or months every year for conservation, safety or environmental reasons; dates are listed on the National Parks' website.

A detailed guide to Thailand's wildlife and their habitats, a look at the environmental issues, and a list of Thai wildlife charities and volunteer projects are provided in "Contexts".

Rock climbing

The limestone karsts that pepper southern Thailand's Andaman coast make ideal playgrounds for rock-climbers, and the sport has really taken off here in the past fifteen years. Most climbing is centred round East Railay and Ton Sai beaches on Laem Phra Nang in Krabi province, where there are dozens of routes within easy walking distance of tourist bungalows, restaurants and beaches. Offshore Deep Water Soloing – climbing a rock face out at sea, with no ropes, partner or bolts and just the water to break your fall – is also huge round here. Several climbing schools at East Railay and Ton Sai provide instruction (from B1000 per half-day), as well as guides and equipment rental (about B1300 per day for two people). Ko Phi Phi also offers a few routes and a couple of climbing schools, as does the quieter and potentially more interesting Ko Yao Noi and Ko Lao Liang. Climbing is also popular near Chiang Mai, and there are less developed climbing areas on Ko Tao and in Lopburi province. For an introduction to climbing on Railay and elsewhere in south Thailand, see wrailay.com, while Rock Climbing in Thailand and King Climbers: Thailand Route Guide Book are regularly updated guidebooks that concentrate on Railay, Ton Sai and the islands.

Sea kayaking and whitewater rafting

Sea kayaking is also centred around Thailand's Andaman coast, where the limestone outcrops, sea caves, hongs (hidden lagoons), mangrove swamps and picturesque shorelines of Ao Phang Nga in particular make for rewarding paddling. Kayaking day-trips around Ao Phang Nga can be arranged from any resort in Phuket, at Khao Lak, at all Krabi beaches and islands, and on Ko Yao Noi; multi-day kayaking expeditions are also possible. Over on Ko Samui, Blue Stars organize kayaking trips around the picturesque islands of the Ang Thong National Marine Park, while Kayak Chang offers half- to seven-day trips around Ko Chang. Many bungalows at other beach resorts have free kayaks or rent them out (from B100/hr) for casual, independent coastal exploration.

You can go river kayaking and whitewater rafting on several rivers in north, west and south Thailand. Some stretches of these rivers can run quite fast, particularly during the rainy season from July to November, but there are plenty of options for novices too. The best time is from October through February; during the hot season (March–June), many rivers run too low. The most popular whitewater-rafting rivers include the Umphang and Mae Khlong rivers near Umphang and the Pai River near Pai. Gentler rafting excursions take place as part of organized treks in the north, as well as on the River Kwai and its tributaries near Kanchanaburi, on the Kok River from Tha Ton, and at Mae Hong Son and Pai. Southwest of Chiang Mai, rafts can be rented from the adjacent national park headquarters for trips in Ob Luang Gorge.

Trekking

Trekking in the mountains of north Thailand differs from trekking in most other parts of the world in that the emphasis is not primarily on the scenery but on the region's inhabitants. Northern Thailand's hill tribes, now numbering over 800,000 people living in around 3500 villages, have preserved their subsistence-oriented way of life with comparatively little change over thousands of years (see The hill tribes). In recent years, the term mountain people (a translation of the Thai chao khao) is increasingly used as a less condescending way to describe them; since these groups have no chief, they are technically not tribes. While some of the villages are near enough to a main road to be reached on a day-trip from a major town, to get to the other, more traditional villages usually entails joining a guided party for a few days, roughing it in a different place each night. For most visitors, however, these hardships are far outweighed by the experience of encountering peoples of so different a culture, travelling through beautiful tropical countryside and tasting the excitement of elephant riding and river rafting.

On any trek you are necessarily confronted by the ethics of your role. About a hundred thousand travellers now go trekking in Thailand each year, the majority heading to certain well-trodden areas such as the Mae Taeng valley, 40km northwest of Chiang Mai, and the hills around the Kok River west of Chiang Rai. Beyond the basic level of disturbance caused by any tourism, this steady flow of trekkers creates pressures for the traditionally insular hill tribes. Foreigners unfamiliar with hill-tribe customs can easily cause grave offence, especially those who go looking for drugs. Though tourism acts as a distraction from their traditional way of life, most tribespeople are genuinely welcoming and hospitable to foreigners, appreciating the contact with Westerners and the minimal material benefits which trekking brings them. Nonetheless, to minimize disruption, it's important to take a responsible attitude when trekking. While it's possible to trek independently from one or two spots such as Cave Lodge near Soppong, the lone trekker will learn very little without a guide as intermediary, and is far more likely to commit an unwitting offence against the local customs; it's best to go with a sensitive and knowledgeable guide who has the welfare of the local people in mind, and follow the basic guidelines on etiquette outlined below. If you don't fancy an organized trek in a group, it's possible to hire a personal guide from an agent, at a cost of about B1000–1500 per day.

The hill tribes are big business in northern Thailand: in Chiang Mai there are hundreds of agencies, which between them cover just about all the trekkable areas in the north. Chiang Rai is the second-biggest trekking centre, and agencies can also be found in Nan, Mae Sariang, Mae Hong Son, Pai, Chiang Dao, Tha Ton and Mae Salong, which usually arrange treks only to the villages in their immediate area. Guided trekking on a smaller scale than in the north is available in Umphang, Kanchanaburi and Sangkhlaburi.

The basics

The cool, dry season from November to February is the best time for treks, which can be as short as two days or as long as ten, but are typically of three or four days' duration. The standard size of a group is between five and twelve people; being part of a small group is preferable, enabling you to strike a more informative relationship with your guides and with the villagers. Everybody in the group usually sleeps on a mattress in the village's guest hut, with a guide cooking communal meals, for which some ingredients are brought from outside and others are found locally.

Each trek usually follows a regular itinerary established by the agency, although they can sometimes be customized, especially for smaller groups and with agencies in the smaller towns. Some itineraries are geared towards serious hikers while others go at a much gentler pace, but on all treks much of the walking will be up and down steep forested hills, often under a burning sun, so a reasonable level of fitness is required. Many treks now include a ride on an elephant and a trip on a bamboo raft – exciting to the point of being dangerous if the river is running fast. The typical three-day, two-night trek costs about B1600–3000 in Chiang Mai (including transport, accommodation, food and guide), sometimes less in other towns, much less without rafting and elephant-riding.

Choosing a trek

There are several features to look out for when choosing a trek. If you want to trek with a small group, get an assurance from your agency that you won't be tagged onto a larger group. Make sure the trek has at least two guides – a leader and a back-marker; some trekkers have been known to get lost for days after becoming separated from the rest of the group. Check exactly when the trek starts and ends and ask about transport to and from base; most treks begin with a pick-up ride out of town, but on rare occasions the trip can entail a long public bus ride. If at all possible, meet and chat with the other trekkers in advance, as well as the guides, who should speak reasonable English and know about hill-tribe culture, especially the details of etiquette in each village. Finally, ask what meals will be included, check how much walking is involved per day and get a copy of the route map to gauge the terrain.

While everybody and their grandmother act as agents, only a few know their guides personally, so choose a reputable agent or guesthouse. When picking an agent, you should check whether they and their guides have licences and certificates from the Tourist Authority of Thailand, which they should be able to show you: this ensures at least a minimum level of training, and provides some comeback in case of problems. Word of mouth is often the best recommendation, so if you hear of a good outfit, try it. Each trek should be registered with the tourist police, stating the itinerary, the duration and the participants, in case the party encounters any trouble – it's worth checking with the agency that the trek has been registered with the tourist police before departure.

What to take

The right clothing is the first essential on any trek. Strong boots with ankle protection are the best footwear, although in the dry season training shoes are adequate. Wear thin, loose clothes – long trousers should be worn to protect against thorns and, in the wet season, leeches – and a hat, and cover your arms if you're prone to sunburn. Antiseptic, antihistamine cream, anti-diarrhoea medicine and insect repellent are essential, as is a mosquito net – check if one will be provided where you're staying. At least two changes of clothing are needed, plus a sarong or towel (women in particular should bring a sarong to wash or change underneath).

If you're going on an organized trek, water is usually provided by the guide, as well as a small backpack. Blankets or, preferably, a sleeping bag are also supplied, but might not be warm enough in the cool season, when night-time temperatures can dip to freezing; you should bring at least a sweater, and perhaps buy a cheap, locally made balaclava to be sure of keeping the chill off.

It's wise not to take anything valuable with you; most guesthouses in trekking-oriented places like Chiang Mai have safes and left-luggage rooms.

Travelling with children

Despite the relative lack of child-centred attractions in Thailand, there's plenty to appeal to families, both on the beach and inland, and Thais are famously welcoming to young visitors.

Of all the beach resorts in the country, two of the most family friendly are the islands of Ko Samui and Ko Lanta. Both have plenty of on-the-beach accommodation for mid- and upper-range budgets, and lots of easy-going open-air shorefront restaurants so that adults can eat in relative peace while kids play within view. Both islands also offer many day-tripping activities, from elephant riding to snorkelling. Phuket is another family favourite, though shorefront accommodation here is at a premium; there are also scores of less mainstream alternatives. In many beach resorts older kids will be able to go kayaking or learn rock climbing, and many dive centres will teach the PADI children's scuba courses on request: the Bubblemaker programme is open to 8- and 9-year-olds and the Discover Scuba Diving day is designed for anyone 10 and over.

Inland, the many national parks and their waterfalls and caves are good for days out, and there are lots of opportunities to go rafting and elephant riding. Kanchanaburi is a rewarding centre for all these, with the added plus that many of the town's guesthouses are set round decent-sized lawns. Chiang Mai is another great hub for all the above and also offers boat trips, an attractive, modern zoo and aquarium, the chance to watch umbrella-makers and other craftspeople at work, and, in the Mae Sa valley, many family-oriented attractions, such as the botanical gardens and butterfly farms. Bangkok has several child-friendly theme parks and activity centres (see Bangkok for kids).

Should you be in Thailand in January, your kids will be able to join in the free entertainments and activities staged all over the country on National Children's Day (Wan Dek), which is held on the second

Saturday of January. They also get free entry to zoos that day, and free rides on public buses.

Hotels and transport

Many of the expensive hotels listed in this guide allow one or two under-12s to share their parents' room for free, as long as no extra bedding is required. It's often possible to cram two adults and two children into the double rooms in budget and mid-range hotels (as opposed to guesthouses), as beds in these places are usually big enough for two. An increasing number of guesthouses now offer three-person rooms, and may even provide special family accommodation. Decent cots are available free in the bigger hotels, and in some smaller ones (though cots in these places can be a bit grotty), and top and mid-range rooms often come with a small fridge. Many hotels can also provide a babysitting service.

Few museums or transport companies offer student reductions, but in some cases children get discounts. One of the more bizarre provisos is the State Railway's regulation that a child aged 3 to 12 qualifies for half-fare only if under 150cm tall; some stations have a measuring scale painted onto the ticket-hall wall. Most domestic airlines charge ten percent of the full fare for under-2s, and fifty percent for under-12s.

Other practicalities

Although most Thai babies don't wear them, disposable nappies (diapers) are sold at convenience stores, pharmacies and supermarkets in big resorts and sizeable towns; for stays on lonely islands, consider bringing some washable ones as back-up. A changing mat is another necessity as there are few public toilets in Thailand, let alone ones with baby facilities (though posh hotels are always a useful option). International brands of powdered milk are available throughout the country, and brand-name baby food is sold in big towns and resorts, though some parents find restaurant-cooked rice and bananas go down just as well. Thai women do not breastfeed in public.

For touring, child-carrier backpacks are ideal. Opinions are divided on whether or not it's worth bringing a buggy or three-wheeled stroller. Where they exist, Thailand's pavements are bumpy at best, and there's an almost total absence of ramps; sand is especially difficult for buggies, though less so for three-wheelers. Buggies and strollers do, however, come in handy for feeding and even bedding small children, as highchairs and cots are only provided in more upmarket restaurants and hotels. You can buy buggies fairly cheaply in most towns, but if you bring your own and then wish you hadn't, most hotels and guesthouses will keep it for you until you leave. Bring an appropriately sized mosquito net if necessary or buy one locally in any department store; a mini sun tent for the beach is also useful. Taxis and car-rental companies almost never provide baby car seats, and even if you bring your own you'll often find there are no seatbelts to strap them in with. Most department stores have dedicated kids' sections selling everything from bottles to dummies. There are even several Mothercare outlets in Bangkok.

Hazards

Even more than their parents, children need protecting from the sun, unsafe drinking water, heat and unfamiliar food. Consider packing a jar of a favourite spread so that you can always rely on toast if all else fails to please. As with adults, you should be careful about unwashed fruit and salads and about dishes that have been left uncovered for a long time. As diarrhoea could be dangerous for a child, rehydration solutions (see Worms and flukes) are vital if your child goes down with it. Other significant hazards include thundering traffic; huge waves, strong currents and jellyfish; and the sun – not least because many beaches offer only limited shade, if at all. Sunhats, sunblock and waterproof suntan lotions are essential, and can be bought in the major resorts. You should also make sure, if possible, that your child is aware of the dangers of rabies; keep children away from animals, especially dogs and monkeys, and ask your medical advisor about rabies jabs.

Information and advice

Nancy Chandler's Family Travel wnancychandler.net/travelwkids.asp. Plenty of unusual ideas on Thai-style entertainment for kids, plus tips, links and Thailand-themed kids' books.

Thailand 4 Kids wthailand4kids.com. Lots of advice on the practicalities of family holidays in Thailand.

Travel essentials

Charities and volunteer projects

Reassured by the plethora of well-stocked shopping plazas, efficient services and apparent abundance in the rice fields, it is easy to forget that life is extremely hard for many people in Thailand. Countless charities work with Thailand's many poor and disadvantaged communities: listed below are a few that would welcome help in some way from visitors. The website of the Bangkok Post also carries an extensive list of charitable foundations and projects in Thailand at wbangkokpost.com/outlookwecare. Longer-term placements, volunteer jobs on charitable wildlife projects and organized holidays that feature community-based programmes are also available (see Internet, National parks and A better kind of travel).

Baan Unrak, Home of Joy Sangkhlaburi wbaanunrak.org. Works with ethnic-minority refugee women and children from Burma. Visitors and volunteers welcome.

Foundation to Encourage the Potential of Disabled Persons Chiang Mai wassistdisabled.org. This foundation provides, among other things, free wheelchairs, home visits and residential care for disabled people. Volunteers, donations and sponsorships for wheelchairs and severely disabled children are sought.

Children's World Academy Kapong, near Khao Lak t087 271 2552, wyaowawit.com. Set in quiet countryside on the Takua Pa–Phang Nga road, Yaowawit School was set up for tsunami orphans and socially disadvantaged children. It accepts donations, volunteer teachers and guests who wish to stay at its lodge, a hospitality training centre.

Hill Area and Community Development Foundation Chiang Rai wnaturalfocus-cbt.com. Aiming to help hill tribes in dealing with problems such as environmental management, HIV/AIDS, child and drug abuse, the foundation has set up a community-based tourism company, Natural Focus, to offer mountain-life tours, volunteer opportunities and study and work programmes.

Human Development Foundation 100/11 Kae Ha Klong Toey 4, Thanon Damrongratthaphipat, Klong Toey, Bangkok t02 671 5313, wmercycentre.org. Founded in 1973, Father Joe Maier's organization provides education and support for Bangkok's street kids and slum-dwellers, as well as for sea gypsies in the south. It now runs two dozen kindergartens in the slums, among many other projects. Contact the centre for information about donations, sponsoring and volunteering. The Slaughterhouse: Stories from Bangkok's Klong Toey Slum gives an eye-opening insight into this often invisible side of Thai life.

Koh Yao Children's Community Center Ko Yao Noi wkoyao-ccc.com. Aims to improve the English-language and lifelong learning skills of islanders on Ko Yao Noi. Visitors, volunteers and donations welcome.

Lifelong Learning Foundation (Thailand) t081 894 6936, wtrangsea.com & wlifelong-learning.org. Promoting nature conservation and the personal development of sea gypsies and other local people in Trang province, this nonprofit organization seeks donations, encourages partnerships with sympathetic overseas organizations, and especially welcomes the custom of tourists at its resorts at Ban Chao Mai and on Ko Mook and Ko Libong, and on its award-winning tours.

Mae Tao Clinic Mae Sot wmaetaoclinic.org. Award-winning health centre providing free care to Burmese refugees. Visitors, donations and volunteers welcome.

The Mirror Foundation 106 Moo 1, Ban Huay Khom, Tambon Mae Yao, Chiang Rai t053 737412, wthemirrorfoundation.org. NGO working with the hill tribes in Chiang Rai province to help combat such issues as drug abuse, erosion of culture and trafficking of women and children; it offers trekking and homestays, as well as a guesthouse in Chiang Rai. Volunteers, interns and donations sought.

The Students' Education Trust (SET) wthaistudentcharity.org. High-school and further education in Thailand is a luxury that the poorest kids cannot afford so many are sent to live in temples instead. The SET helps such kids pursue their education and escape from the poverty trap. Some of their stories are told in Little Angels: The Real-Life Stories of Twelve Thai Novice Monks. SET welcomes donations.

Thai Child Development Foundation Pha To wthaichilddevelopment.org. This small Thai-Dutch-run village project in Chumphon province helps educate, feed and look after needy local children. The foundation welcomes donations of materials and money, takes on volunteers, and has an ecotourism arm (see Ko Samet).

Climate

There are three main seasons in most of Thailand: rainy, caused by the southwest monsoon (the least predictable, but roughly May–Oct); cool (Nov–Feb; felt most distinctly in the far north, but hardly at all in the south); and hot (March–May). The Gulf coast's climate is slightly different: it suffers less from the southwest monsoon, but is then hit by the northeast monsoon, making November its rainiest month.

Costs

Thailand can be a very cheap place to travel. At the bottom of the scale, you can manage on a budget of about B650 (£13/US$20) per day if you're willing to opt for basic accommodation, eat, drink and travel as the locals do, and stay away from the more expensive resorts like Phuket, Ko Samui and Ko Phi Phi – and you'd have to work hard to stick to this daily allowance in Bangkok. On this budget, you'll be spending around B200 for a dorm or shared room (more for a single room), around B200 on three meals (eating mainly at night markets and simple noodle shops, and eschewing beer), and the rest on travel (sticking to the cheaper buses and third-class trains where possible) and incidentals. With extras like air conditioning in rooms, taking the various forms of taxi rather than buses or shared songthaews for cross-town journeys, and a meal and beer in a more touristy restaurant, a day's outlay would look more like B1000 (£20/US$30). Staying in well-equipped, mid-range hotels and eating in the more exclusive restaurants, you should be able to live very comfortably for around B2000 a day (£40/US$60).

Travellers soon get so used to the low cost of living in Thailand that they start bargaining at every available opportunity, much as Thai people do. Although it's expected practice for a lot of commercial transactions, particularly at markets and when hiring tuk-tuks and unmetered taxis (though not in supermarkets or department stores), bargaining is a delicate art that requires humour, tact and patience. If your price is way out of line, the vendor's vehement refusal should be enough to make you increase your offer: never forget that the few pennies or cents you're making such a fuss over will go a lot further in a Thai person's hands than in your own.

It's rare that foreigners can bargain a price down as low as a Thai could, anyway, while two-tier pricing has been made official at government-run sights, as a kind of informal tourist tax: at national parks, for example, foreigners pay up to B400 entry while Thais generally pay just B20. A number of privately owned tourist attractions follow a similar two-tier system, posting an inflated price in English for foreigners and a lower price in Thai for locals.

Big-spending shoppers who are departing via Suvarnabhumi, Chiang Mai, Hat Yai, Ko Samui, Krabi, Pattaya or Phuket airports can save some money by claiming a Value Added Tax refund (wrd.go.th/vrt), though it's a bit of a palaver for seven percent (the current rate of VAT). The total amount of your purchases (gems are excluded) from participating shops needs to be at least B5000 per person, with a minimum of B2000 per shop per day. You'll need to show your passport and fill in an application form (to which original tax invoices need to be attached) at the shop. At the relevant airport, you'll need to show your form and purchases to customs officers before checking in, then make your claim from VAT refund officers – from which fees of at least B100 are deducted.

Crime and personal safety

As long as you keep your wits about you, you shouldn't encounter much trouble in Thailand. Pickpocketing and bag-snatching are two of the main problems – not surprising considering that a huge percentage of the local population scrape by on under US$5 per day – but the most common cause for concern is the number of con-artists who dupe gullible tourists into parting with their cash. There are various Thai laws that tourists need to be aware of, particularly regarding passports, the age of consent and smoking in public.

Theft

To prevent theft, most travellers prefer to carry their valuables with them at all times, but it's often possible to use a locker in a hotel or guesthouse – the safest are those that require your own padlock, as there are occasional reports of valuables being stolen by hotel staff. Padlock your luggage when leaving it in hotel or guesthouse rooms, as well as when consigning it to storage or taking it on public transport. Padlocks also come in handy as extra security on your room, particularly on the doors of beachfront bamboo huts.

Theft from some long-distance buses is also a problem, with the majority of reported incidents taking place on the temptingly cheap overnight buses run by private companies direct from Bangkok's Thanon Khao San (as opposed to those that depart from the government bus stations) to destinations such as Chiang Mai and southern beach resorts. The best solution is to go direct from the bus stations (see Ordinary and second-class).

Personal safety

On any bus, private or government, and on any train journey, never keep anything of value in luggage that is stored out of your sight and be wary of accepting food and drink from fellow passengers as it may be drugged. This might sound paranoid, but there have been enough drug-muggings for TAT to publish a specific warning about the problem. Drinks can also be spiked in bars and clubs; at full moon parties on Ko Pha Ngan this has led to sexual assaults against farang women, while prostitutes sometimes spike drinks so they can steal from their victim's room.

Violent crime against tourists is not common, but it does occur, and there have been several serious attacks on women travellers in recent years. However, bearing in mind that fourteen million foreigners visit Thailand every year, the statistical likelihood of becoming a victim is extremely small. Obvious precautions for travellers of either sex include locking accessible windows and doors at night – preferably with your own padlock (doors in many of the simpler guesthouses and beach bungalows are designed for this) – and not travelling alone at night in a taxi or tuk-tuk. Nor should you risk jumping into an unlicensed taxi at the airport in Bangkok at any time of day: there have been some very violent robberies in these, so take the well-marked licensed, metered taxis instead.

Among hazards to watch out for in the natural world, riptides claim a number of tourist lives every year, particularly off Phuket, Ko Chang (Trat), Hua Hin, Cha-am, Rayong, Pattaya and the Ko Samui archipelago during stormy periods of the monsoon season, so always pay attention to warning signs and red flags, and always ask locally if unsure. Jellyfish can be a problem on any coast, especially just after a storm (see Other bites and stings).

Unfortunately, it is also necessary for female tourists to think twice about spending time alone with a monk, as not all men of the cloth uphold the Buddhist precepts and there have been rapes and murders committed by men wearing the saffron robes of the monkhood.

Though unpalatable and distressing, Thailand's high-profile sex industry is relatively unthreatening for Western women, with its energy focused exclusively on farang men; it's also quite easily avoided, being contained within certain pockets of the capital and a couple of beach resorts.

As for harassment from men, it's hard to generalize, but most Western women find it less of a problem in Thailand than they do back home. Outside the main tourist spots, you're more likely to be of interest as a foreigner rather than a woman and, if travelling alone, as an object of concern rather than of sexual aggression.

Regional issues

It's advisable to travel with a guide if you're going off the main roads in certain border areas or, at the very least, to take advice before setting off. As these regions are generally covered in dense unmapped jungle, you shouldn't find yourself alone in the area anyway, but the main stretches to watch are the immediate vicinity of the Burmese border, where fighting on the other side of the border now and again spills over and where there are occasional clashes between Thai security forces and illegal traffickers; and the border between Cambodia and southern Isaan, which is littered with unexploded mines and which has seen recent clashes between the Thai and Cambodian armies over the disputed line of the border, especially at Khao Phra Viharn (Preah Vihear).

Because of the violence in the deep south, all Western governments are currently advising against travel to or through the border provinces of Songkhla, Yala, Pattani and Narathiwat, unless essential (see Travel warning). For up-to-the-minute advice on current political trouble-spots, consult your government's travel advisory.

Scams

Despite the best efforts of guidebook writers, TAT and the Thai tourist police, countless travellers to Thailand get scammed every year. Nearly all scams are easily avoided if you're on your guard against anyone who makes an unnatural effort to befriend you. We have outlined the main scams in the relevant sections of this guide, but con-artists are nothing if not creative, so if in doubt walk away at the earliest opportunity. The worst areas for scammers are the busy tourist centres, including many parts of Bangkok and the main beach resorts.

Many tuk-tuk drivers earn most of their living through securing commissions from tourist-oriented shops; this is especially true in Bangkok, where they will do their damnedest to get you to go to a gem shop. The most common tactic is for drivers to pretend that the Grand Palace or other major sight you intended to visit is closed for the day (see City of angels), and to then offer to take you on a round-city tour instead, perhaps even for free. The tour will invariably include a visit to a gem shop. The easiest way to avoid all this is to take a metered taxi; if you're fixed on taking a tuk-tuk, ignore any tuk-tuk that is parked up or loitering and be firm about where you want to go.

Self-styled tourist guides, touts and anyone else who might introduce themselves as students or business people and offer to take you somewhere of interest, or invite you to meet their family, are often the first piece of bait in a well-honed chain of con-artists. If you bite, chances are you'll end up either at a gem shop or in a gambling den, or, at best, at a tour operator or hotel that you had not planned to patronize.

This is not to say that you should never accept an invitation from a local person, but be extremely wary of doing so following a street encounter in Bangkok or the resorts. Tourist guides' ID cards are easily faked.

For many of these characters, the goal is to get you inside a dodgy gem shop, nearly all of which are located in Bangkok, but the bottom line is that if you are not experienced at buying and trading in valuable gems you will definitely be ripped off, possibly even to the tune of several thousand dollars. Check the 2Bangkok website's account of a typical gem scam (w2bangkok.com/2bangkok-scams-sapphire.html) before you shell out any cash at all.

A less common but potentially more frightening scam involves a similar cast of warm-up artists leading tourists into a gambling game. The scammers invite their victim home on an innocent-sounding pretext, get out a pack of cards, and then set about fleecing the incomer in any number of subtle ways. Often this can be especially scary as the venue is likely to be far from hotels or recognizable landmarks. You're unlikely to get any sympathy from police, as gambling is illegal in Thailand.

An increasing number of travel agents in tourist centres all over the country are trying to pass themselves off as official government tourist information offices, displaying nothing but "TOURIST INFORMATION" on their shop signs or calling themselves names like "T&T" (note that the actual TAT, the Tourism Authority of Thailand, does not book hotels or sell any kind of travel ticket). Fakers like this are more likely to sell you tickets for services that turn out to be sub-standard or even not to exist. A word of warning also about jet skis: operators, who usually ask for a passport as guarantee, will often try to charge renters exorbitant amounts of money for any minor damage they claim to find on return.

Age restrictions and other laws

Thai law requires that tourists carry their original passports at all times, though sometimes it's more practical to carry a photocopy and keep the original locked in a safety deposit. The age of consent is 15, but the law allows anyone under the age of 18, or their parents, to file charges in retrospect even if they consented to sex at the time. It is against the law to have sex with a prostitute who is under 18. It is illegal for under-18s to buy cigarettes or to drive and you must be 20 or over to buy alcohol or be allowed into a bar or club (ID checks are sometimes enforced in Bangkok). It is illegal for anyone to gamble in Thailand (though many do).

Smoking in public is widely prohibited. The ban covers all air-conditioned public buildings (including restaurants, bars and clubs) and air-conditioned trains, buses and planes and even extends to parks and the street; violators may be subject to a B2000 fine. Dropping cigarette butts, littering and spitting in public places can also earn you a B2000 fine. There are fines for overstaying your visa (see Border runs, extensions and re-entry permits), working without a permit, not wearing a motorcycle helmet and violating other traffic laws.

Drugs

Drug-smuggling carries a maximum penalty in Thailand of death and dealing drugs will get you anything from four years to life in a Thai prison; penalties depend on the drug and the amount involved. Travellers caught with even the smallest amount of drugs at airports and international borders are prosecuted for trafficking, and no one charged with trafficking offences gets bail. Heroin, amphetamines, LSD and ecstasy are classed as Category 1 drugs and carry the most severe penalties: even possession of Category 1 drugs for personal use can result in a life sentence. Away from international borders, most foreigners arrested in possession of small amounts of cannabis are released on bail, then fined and deported, but the law is complex and prison sentences are possible.

Despite occasional royal pardons, don't expect special treatment as a farang: you only need to read one of the first-hand accounts by foreign former prisoners (see Travelogues) or read the blogs at wthaiprisonlife.com to get the picture. The police actively look for tourists doing drugs, reportedly searching people regularly and randomly on Thanon Khao San, for example. They have the power to order a urine test if they have reasonable grounds for suspicion, and even a positive result for marijuana consumption could lead to a year's imprisonment. Be wary also of being shopped by a farang or local dealer keen to earn a financial reward for a successful bust (there are setups at the Ko Pha Ngan full moon parties, for example), or having substances slipped into your luggage (simple enough to perpetrate unless all fastenings are secured with padlocks).

If you are arrested, ask for your embassy to be contacted immediately (see Gem scams), which is your right under Thai law, and embassy staff will talk you through procedures; the website of the British Embassy in Thailand also posts useful information, including a list of English-speaking lawyers, at wukinthailand.fco.gov.uk/en/help-for-british-nationals. The British charity Prisoners Abroad (wprisonersabroad.org.uk) carries a detailed survival guide on its website, which outlines what to expect if arrested in Thailand, from the point of apprehension through trial and conviction to life in a Thai jail; if contacted, the charity may also be able to offer direct support to a British citizen facing imprisonment in a Thai jail.

Customs regulations

The duty-free allowance on entry to Thailand is 200 cigarettes (or 250g of tobacco) and a litre of spirits or wine.

To export antiques or newly cast Buddha images from Thailand, you need to have a licence granted by the Fine Arts Department (the export of antique Buddhas is forbidden). Licences can be obtained for example through the Office of Archeology and National Museums, 81/1 Thanon Si Ayutthaya (near the National Library), Bangkok (t02 628 5032), or through the national museums in Chiang Mai or Phuket. Applications take at least three working days in Bangkok, generally more in the provinces, and need to be accompanied by the object itself, some evidence of its rightful possession, two postcard-sized colour photos of it, taken face-on and against a white background, and photocopies of the applicant's passport; furthermore, if the object is a Buddha image, the passport photocopies need to be certified by your embassy in Bangkok. Some antiques shops can organize all this for you.

Departure taxes

International and domestic departure taxes are included in the price of all tickets.

Electricity

Mains electricity is supplied at 220 volts AC and is available at all but the most remote villages and basic beach huts. Where electricity is supplied by generators and/or solar power, for example on the smaller, less populated islands, it is often rationed to evenings only. If you're packing phone and camera chargers, a hair dryer, laptop or other appliance, you'll need to take a set of travel-plug adapters with you as several plug types are commonly in use, most usually with two round pins, but also with two flat-blade pins, and sometimes with both options.

Entry requirements

There are three main entry categories for visitors to Thailand; for all of them, under International Air Travel Association rules, your passport should be valid for at least six months. As visa requirements are subject to frequent change, you should always consult before departure a Thai embassy or consulate, a reliable travel agent, or the Thai Ministry of Foreign Affairs' website at wmfa.go.th/web/2637.php. For further, unofficial but usually reliable, details on all visa matters, go to wthaivisa.com and especially their various moderated forums.

Most Western passport holders (that includes citizens of the UK, Ireland, the US, Canada, Australia, New Zealand and South Africa) are allowed to enter the country for short stays without having to apply for a visa – officially termed the tourist visa exemption. You'll be granted a thirty-day stay at an international airport but only fifteen days at an overland border; the period of stay will be stamped into your passport by immigration officials upon entry. You're supposed to be able to somehow show proof of means of living while in the country (B10,000 per person, B20,000 per family), and in theory you may be put back on the next plane without it or sent back to get a sixty-day tourist visa from the nearest Thai embassy, but this is unheard of. You are also required to show proof of tickets to leave Thailand again within the allotted time. This is rarely checked by Thai immigration authorities, though there have been a few cases recently, mostly at the Cambodian border. However, if you have a one-way air ticket to Thailand and no evidence of onward travel arrangements, it's best to buy a tourist visa in advance: some airlines will stop you boarding the plane without one, as they would be liable for flying you back to your point of origin if you did happen to be stopped.

If you're fairly certain you may want to stay longer than fifteen/thirty days, then from the outset you should apply for a sixty-day tourist visa from a Thai embassy or consulate, accompanying your application – which generally takes several days to process – with your passport and one or two photos. The sixty-day visa currently costs, for example, £25 in the UK; multiple-entry versions are available, costing £25 per entry, which may be handy if you're going to be leaving and re-entering Thailand. Ordinary tourist visas are valid for three months, ie you must enter Thailand within three months of the visa being issued by the Thai embassy or consulate, while multiple-entry versions are valid for six months. Visa application forms can be downloaded from, for example, the Thai Ministry of Foreign Affairs' website.

Thai embassies also consider applications for ninety-day non-immigrant visas (£50, in the UK for example, for single entry, £125 multiple-entry) as long as you can offer a reason for your visit, such as study, business or visiting family/friends (there are different categories of non-immigrant visa for which different levels of proof are needed). As it can be a hassle to organize a ninety-day visa, it's generally easier to apply for a thirty-day extension to your sixty-day visa once inside Thai borders.

It's not a good idea to overstay your visa limits. Once you're at the airport or the border, you'll have to pay a fine of B500 per day before you can leave Thailand. More importantly, however, if you're in the country with an expired visa and you get involved with police or immigration officials for any reason, however trivial, they are obliged to take you to court, possibly imprison you, and deport you.

Border runs, extensions and re-entry permits

Setting aside the caveats about proof of funds and onward tickets (see Customs regulations), it's generally easy to get a new fifteen-day tourist visa exemption by hopping across the border into a neighbouring country and back. Such tourist visa exemptions can be extended within Thailand for a further seven days, sixty-day tourist visas for a further thirty days, at the discretion of immigration officials; extensions cost B1900 and are issued over the counter at immigration offices (kaan khao muang; t1111 for 24hr information in English, wimmigration.go.th) in nearly every provincial capital – most offices ask for one or two photos as well, plus one or two photocopies of the main pages of your passport including your Thai departure card, arrival stamp and visa. Many Khao San tour agents offer to get your visa extension for you, but beware: some are reportedly faking the stamps, which could get you into serious trouble. Immigration offices also issue re-entry permits (B1000 single re-entry, B3800 multiple) if you want to leave the country and come back again while maintaining the validity of your existing visa.

Thai embassies and consulates abroad

For a full listing of Thai diplomatic missions abroad, consult the Thai Ministry of Foreign Affairs' website at wmfa.go.th/web/2712.php; their other site, wthaiembassy.org, has links to the websites of most of the offices below.

Australia 111 Empire Circuit, Yarralumla, Canberra ACT 2600 t02/6206 0100; plus consulate at 131 Macquarrie St, Sydney, NSW 2000 t02/9241 2542–3.

Burma 94 Pyay Rd, Dagon Township, Rangoon t01/226721.

Cambodia 196 Preah Norodom Blvd, Sangkat Tonle Bassac, Khan Chamcar Mon, Phnom Penh t023/726306–10.

Canada 180 Island Park Drive, Ottawa, ON, K1Y 0A2 t613/722-4444; plus consulate at 1040 Burrard St, Vancouver, BC, V6Z 2R9 t604/687-1143.

Laos Vientiane: embassy at Avenue Kaysone Phomvihane, Saysettha District t021/214581–2, consular section at Unit 15 Bourichane Rd, Ban Phone Si Nuan, Muang Si Sattanak t021/453916; plus consulate at Khanthabouly District, Savannakhet Province, PO Box 513 t041/212373.

Malaysia 206 Jalan Ampang, 50450 Kuala Lumpur t03/2148 8222; plus consulates at 4426 Jalan Pengkalan Chepa, 15400 Kota Bharu t09/748 2545; and 1 Jalan Tunku Abdul Rahman, 10350 Penang t04/226 9484.

New Zealand 110 Molesworth St, Thorndon, Wellington t04/476 8616.

Singapore 370 Orchard Rd, Singapore 238870 t6737 2158.

South Africa 428 Pretorius/Hill St, Arcadia, Pretoria 0083 t012/342 5470.

UK & Ireland 29–30 Queens Gate, London SW7 5JB t020/7589 2944. Visa applications by post are not accepted here, but can be sent to various honorary consulates, including those in Hull (w

thaiconsul-uk.com) and Dublin (wthaiconsulateireland.com).

US 1024 Wisconsin Ave NW, Suite 401, Washington, DC 20007 t202/944-3600; plus consulates at 700 North Rush St, Chicago, IL 60611 t312/664-3129; 611 North Larchmont Blvd, 2nd Floor, Los Angeles, CA 90004 t323/962-9574; and 351 E 52nd St, New York, NY 10022 t212/754-1770.

Vietnam 63–65 Hoang Dieu St, Hanoi t04/3823-5092–4; plus consulate at 77 Tran Quoc Thao St, District 3, Ho Chi Minh City t08/3932-7637–8.

Gay and lesbian Thailand

Buddhist tolerance and a national abhorrence of confrontation and victimization combine to make Thai society relatively tolerant of homosexuality, if not exactly positive about same-sex relationships. Most Thais are extremely private and discreet about being gay, generally pursuing a "don't ask, don't tell" understanding with their family. The majority of people are horrified by the idea of gay-bashing and generally regard it as unthinkable to spurn a child or relative for being gay.

Hardly any Thai celebrities are out, yet the predilections of several respected social, political and entertainment figures are widely known and accepted. There is no mention of homosexuality at all in Thai law, which means that the age of consent for gay sex is fifteen, the same as for heterosexuals. However, this also means that gay rights are not protected under Thai law.

Although excessively physical displays of affection are frowned upon for both heterosexuals and homosexuals, Western gay couples should get no hassle about being seen together in public – it's much more acceptable, and common, in fact, for friends of the same sex (gay or not) to walk hand-in-hand, than for heterosexual couples to do so.

Transvestites (known as katoey or "ladyboys") and transsexuals are also a lot more visible in Thailand than in the West. You'll find cross-dressers doing ordinary jobs, even in small upcountry towns, and there are a number of transvestites and transsexuals in the public eye too – including national volleyball stars and champion muay thai boxers. The government tourist office vigorously promotes the transvestite cabarets in Pattaya, Phuket and Bangkok, all of which are advertised as family entertainment. Katoey also regularly appear as characters in soap operas, TV comedies and films, where they are depicted as stereotyped but harmless figures of fun. Richard Totman's The Third Sex offers an interesting insight into Thai katoey, their experiences in society and public attitudes towards them.

The scene

Thailand's gay scene is mainly focused on mainstream venues like karaoke bars, restaurants, massage parlours, gyms, saunas and escort agencies. For the sake of discretion, gay venues are usually intermingled with straight ones. Bangkok, Phuket and Pattaya have the biggest concentrations of farang-friendly gay bars and clubs, and Chiang Mai has an established bar scene. For a detailed guide to the gay and lesbian scene throughout the country, see the Utopia Guide to Thailand by John Goss, which can be ordered or downloaded as an e-book via wutopia-asia.com.

Thai lesbians generally eschew the word lesbian, which in Thailand is associated with male fantasies, instead referring to themselves as either tom (for tomboy) or dee (for lady). There are hardly any dedicated tom-dee venues in Thailand, but we've listed established ones where possible; unless otherwise specified, gay means male throughout this guide.

The farang-oriented gay sex industry is a tiny but highly visible part of Thailand's gay scene. With its tawdry floor shows and host services, it bears a dispiriting resemblance to the straight sex trade, and is similarly most active in Bangkok, Pattaya, Patong (on Phuket) and Chiang Mai. Like their female counterparts in the heterosexual fleshpots, many of the boys working in the gay sex bars that dominate these districts are underage; note that anyone caught having sex with a prostitute below the age of 18 faces imprisonment. A significant number of gay prostitutes are gay by economic necessity rather than by inclination. As with the straight sex scene, we do not list commercial gay sex bars in the guide.

Information and contacts for gay travellers

Bangkok Lesbian wbangkoklesbian.com. Organized by foreign lesbians living in Thailand, Bangkok Lesbian hosts regular parties and posts general info and listings of the capital's lesbian-friendly hangouts on its website.

Dreaded Ned's wdreadedned.com. Guide to the scene in Thailand that's most useful for its what's-on listings.

Gay People in Thailand wthaivisa.com/forum/Gay-People-Thailand-f27.html. Popular forum for gay expats.

Utopia wutopia-asia.com and wutopia-asia.com/womthai.htm. Asia's best gay and lesbian website lists clubs, events, accommodation, tour operators and organizations for gays and lesbians and has useful links to other sites in Asia and the rest of the world.

Health

Although Thailand's climate, wildlife and cuisine present Western travellers with fewer health worries than in many Asian destinations, it's as well to know in advance what the risks might be, and what preventive or curative measures you should take.

For a start, there's no need to bring huge supplies of non-prescription medicines with you, as Thai pharmacies (raan khai yaa; typically open daily 8.30am–8pm) are well stocked with local and international branded medicaments, and of course they are generally much less expensive than at home. Nearly all pharmacies are run by trained English-speaking pharmacists, who are usually the best people to talk to if your symptoms aren't acute enough to warrant seeing a doctor. The British pharmacy chain, Boots, now has branches in many big cities (see wth.boots.com for locations). These are the best place to stock up on some Western products such as tampons (which Thai women do not use).

Hospital (rong phayabaan) cleanliness and efficiency vary, but generally hygiene and healthcare standards are good and the ratio of medical staff to patients is considerably higher than in most parts of the West. As with head pharmacists, doctors speak English. Several Bangkok hospitals are highly regarded (see Directory), and all provincial capitals have at least one hospital: if you need to get to one, ask at your accommodation for advice on, and possibly transport to, the nearest or most suitable. In the event of a major health crisis, get someone to contact your embassy (see Antiques) and insurance company – it may be best to get yourself transported to Bangkok or even home.

There have been outbreaks of Avian Influenza (bird flu) in domestic poultry and wild birds in Thailand (most recently in 2008) which have led to a small number of human fatalities, believed to have arisen through close contact with infected poultry. There has been no evidence of human-to-human transmission in Thailand, and the risk to humans is believed to be very low. However, as a precaution, you should avoid visiting live-animal markets and other places where you may come into close contact with birds, and ensure that poultry and egg dishes are thoroughly cooked.

Inoculations

There are no compulsory inoculation requirements for people travelling to Thailand from the West, but you should consult a doctor or other health professional, preferably at least four weeks in advance of your trip, for the latest information on recommended immunizations. In addition to making sure that your recommended immunizations for life in your home country are up to date, most doctors strongly advise vaccinations or boosters against tetanus, diphtheria, hepatitis A and, in many cases, typhoid, and in some cases they might also recommend protecting yourself against Japanese encephalitis, rabies and hepatitis B. There is currently no vaccine against malaria. If you forget to have all your inoculations before leaving home, or don't leave yourself sufficient time, you can get them in Bangkok at, for example, the Thai Red Cross Society's Queen Saovabha Institute or Global Doctor.

Mosquito-borne diseases

Mosquitoes in Thailand spread not only malaria, but also diseases such as dengue fever and the very similar chikungunya fever, especially during the rainy season. The main message, therefore, is to avoid being bitten by mosquitoes. You should smother yourself and your clothes in mosquito repellent containing the chemical compound DEET, reapplying regularly (shops, guesthouses and department stores all over Thailand stock it, but if you want the highest-strength repellent, or convenient roll-ons or sprays, do your shopping before you leave home). DEET is strong stuff, and if you have sensitive skin, a natural alternative is citronella (available in the UK as Mosi-guard), made from a blend of eucalyptus oils; the Thai version is made with lemon grass.

At night you should sleep either under a mosquito net sprayed with DEET or in a bedroom with mosquito screens across the windows (or in an enclosed air-con room). Accommodation in tourist spots nearly always provides screens or a net (check both for holes), but if you're planning to go way off the beaten track or want the security of having your own mosquito net just in case, wait until you get to Bangkok to buy one, where department stores sell them for much less than you'd pay in the West. Plug-in insecticide vaporizers, insect room sprays and mosquito coils – also widely available in Thailand – help keep the insects at bay; electronic "buzzers" are useless.

Malaria

Thailand is malarial, with the disease being carried by mosquitoes that bite from dusk to dawn, but the risks involved vary across the country.

There is a significant risk of malaria, mainly in rural and forested areas, in a narrow strip along the borders with Cambodia (excluding Ko Chang), Laos and Burma (the highest-risk area, including the countryside around Mae Hong Son, but excluding, for example, Chiang Mai, Chiang Rai and Kanchanaburi towns, and resorts and road and rail routes along the Gulf coast). Discuss with your travel health adviser which anti-malarial drugs are currently likely to be effective in these areas, as prophylaxis advice can change from year to year.

Elsewhere in Thailand the risk of malaria is considered to be so low that anti-malarial tablets are not advised.

The signs of malaria are often similar to flu, but are very variable. The incubation period for malignant malaria, which can be fatal, is usually 7–28 days, but it can take up to a year for symptoms of the benign form to occur. The most important symptom is a raised temperature of at least

38°C beginning a week or more after the first potential exposure to malaria: if you suspect anything, go to a hospital or clinic immediately.

Dengue fever

Dengue fever, a debilitating and occasionally fatal viral disease that is particularly prevalent during and just after the rainy season, is on the increase throughout tropical Asia, and is endemic to many areas of Thailand, with over 115,000 reported cases in 2010. Unlike malaria, dengue fever is spread by mosquitoes that can bite during daylight hours, so you should also use mosquito repellent during the day. Symptoms include fever, headaches, fierce joint and muscle pain ("breakbone fever" is another name for dengue), and possibly a rash, and usually develop between five and eight days after being bitten.

There is no vaccine against dengue fever; the only treatment is lots of rest, liquids and paracetamol (or any other acetaminophen painkiller, not aspirin), though more serious cases may require hospitalization.

Rabies

Rabies is widespread in Thailand, mainly carried by dogs (between four and seven percent of stray dogs in Bangkok are reported to be rabid), but also cats and monkeys. It is transmitted by bites, scratches or even occasionally licks. Dogs are everywhere in Thailand and even if kept as pets they're often not very well cared for; hopefully their mangy appearance will discourage the urge to pat them, as you should steer well clear of them. Rabies is invariably fatal if the patient waits until symptoms begin, though modern vaccines and treatments are very effective and deaths are rare. The important thing is, if you are bitten, licked or scratched by an animal, to vigorously clean the wound with soap and disinfect it, preferably with something containing iodine, and to seek medical advice regarding treatment right away.

Other bites and stings

Thailand's seas are home to a few dangerous creatures that you should look out for, notably jellyfish, which tend to be washed towards the beach by rough seas during the monsoon season but can appear at any time of year. All manner of stinging and non-stinging jellyfish can be found in Thailand – as a general rule, those with the longest tentacles tend to have the worst stings – but reports of serious incidents are rare; ask around at your resort or at a local dive shop to see if there have been any sightings of venomous varieties. You also need to be wary of venomous sea snakes, sea urchins and a couple of less conspicuous species – stingrays, which often lie buried in the sand, and stonefish, whose potentially lethal venomous spikes are easily stepped on because the fish look like stones and lie motionless on the sea bed.

If stung or bitten you should always seek medical advice as soon as possible, but there are a few ways of alleviating the pain or administering your own first-aid in the meantime. If you're stung by a jellyfish, wash the affected area with salt water (not fresh water) and, if possible, with vinegar (failing that, ammonia, citrus fruit juice or even urine may do the trick), and try to remove the fragments of tentacles from the skin with a gloved hand, forceps, thick cloth or credit card. The best way to minimize the risk of stepping on the toxic spines of sea urchins, stingrays and stonefish is to wear thick-soled shoes, though these cannot provide total protection; sea urchin spikes should be removed after softening the skin with ointment, though some people recommend applying urine to help dissolve the spines; for stingray and stonefish stings, alleviate the pain by immersing the wound in hot water while awaiting help.

In the case of a venomous snake bite, don't try sucking out the venom or applying a tourniquet: wrap up and immobilize the bitten limb and try to stay still and calm until medical help arrives; all provincial hospitals in Thailand carry supplies of antivenins.

Some of Thailand's wilder, less developed beaches are plagued by sandflies, tiny, barely visible midges whose bites can trigger an allergic response, leaving big red weals and an unbearable itch, and possible infection if scratched too vigorously. Many islanders say that slathering yourself in (widely available) coconut oil is the best deterrent as sandflies apparently don't like the smell. Applying locally made camphor-based yellow oil (see Coastal Chanthaburi) quells the itch, but you may need to resort to antihistamines for the inflammation. Leeches aren't dangerous but can be a bother when walking in forested areas, especially during and just after the rainy season. The most effective way to get leeches off your skin is to burn them with a lighted cigarette, or douse them in salt; oily suntan lotion or insect repellent sometimes makes them lose their grip and fall off.

Worms and flukes

Worms can be picked up through the soles of your feet, so avoid going barefoot. They can also be ingested by eating undercooked meat, and liver flukes by eating raw or undercooked freshwater fish. Worms which cause schistosomiasis (bilharziasis) by attaching themselves to your bladder or intestines can be found in freshwater rivers and lakes. The risk of contracting this disease is low, but you should avoid swimming in the southern reaches of the Mekong River and in most freshwater lakes.

Digestive problems

By far the most common travellers' complaint in Thailand, digestive troubles are often caused by contaminated food and water, or sometimes just by an overdose of unfamiliar foodstuffs (see Food and drink and Desserts).

Stomach trouble usually manifests itself as simple diarrhoea, which should clear up without medical treatment within three to seven days and is best combated by drinking lots of fluids. If this doesn't work, you're in danger of getting dehydrated and should take some kind of rehydration solution, either a commercial sachet of ORS (oral rehydration solution), sold in all Thai pharmacies, or a do-it-yourself version, which can be made by adding a handful of sugar and a pinch of salt to every litre of boiled or bottled water (soft drinks are not a viable alternative). If you can eat, avoid fatty foods.

Anti-diarrhoeal agents such as Imodium are useful for blocking you up on long bus journeys, but only attack the symptoms and may prolong infections; an antibiotic such as ciprofloxacin, however, can often reduce a typical attack of traveller's diarrhoea to one day. If the diarrhoea persists for a week or more, or if you have blood or mucus in your stools, or an accompanying fever, go to a doctor or hospital.

HIV and AIDS

HIV infection is widespread in Thailand, primarily because of the sex trade. Condoms (meechai) are sold in pharmacies, convenience stores, department stores, hairdressers and even street markets. Due to rigorous screening methods, Thailand's medical blood supply is now considered safe from HIV/AIDS infection.

Medical resources

Canadian Society for International Health t613/241-5785, wcsih.org. Extensive list of travel health centres.

CDC t1-800/232 4636, wcdc.gov/travel. Official US government travel health site.

Hospital for Tropical Diseases Travel Clinic UK wthehtd.org.

International Society for Travel Medicine US t1-404/373-8282, wistm.org. Has a full list of travel health clinics.

MASTA (Medical Advisory Service for Travellers Abroad) UK wmasta.org.

NHS Travel Health Website UK wfitfortravel.scot.nhs.uk.

The Travel Doctor – TMVC t1300/658 844, wtmvc.com.au. Lists travel clinics in Australia, New Zealand and South Africa.

Tropical Medical Bureau Ireland t1850/487 674, wtmb.ie.

Insurance

Most visitors to Thailand will need to take out specialist travel insurance, though you should check exactly what's covered. Insurers will generally not cover travel in Songkhla, Yala, Pattani and Narathiwat provinces in the deep south, as Western governments are currently advising against going to these areas unless it's essential (see Travel warning). Policies generally also exclude so-called dangerous sports unless an extra premium is paid: in Thailand this can mean such things as scuba diving, white-water rafting and trekking.

Other basics

Internet

Internet access is very widespread and very cheap in Thailand. You'll find traveller-oriented internet cafés in every touristed town and resort in the country – there are at least twenty in the Banglamphu district of Bangkok, for example. In untouristed neighbourhoods throughout the country you can always check your email at the ubiquitous online games centres, favourite after-school haunts that are easily spotted from the piles of schoolboy pumps outside the door. Competition keeps prices low: upcountry you could expect to pay as little as B20 per hour, while rates in tourist centres average B1 per minute.

Increasing numbers of budget guesthouses and cheap hotels, especially in Bangkok, offer wi-fi in all or parts of their establishment; all upmarket hotels have it, though rates are sometimes astronomical. Plenty of cafés, restaurants, bars and other locations across the country provide wi-fi, which is usually free to customers. For a list of hot spots nationwide, try wjiwire.com; for free locations, go to wstickmanweekly.com.

Laundry

Guesthouses and cheap hotels all over the country run low-cost, same-day laundry services, though in luxury hotels, it'll cost an arm and a leg. In some places you pay per item, in others you're charged by the kilo (generally around B30–50 per kg); ironing is often included in the price.

Left luggage

Most major train stations have left luggage facilities, where bags can be stored for up to twenty days (around B30–80 per item per day); at bus stations you can usually persuade someone official to look after your stuff for a few hours. Many guesthouses and basic hotels also offer an inexpensive and reliable service, while upmarket hotels should be able to look after your luggage for free. There's also left luggage at Bangkok, Chiang Mai and Phuket international airports (B80–140 per day).

Living in Thailand

The most common source of employment in Thailand is teaching English, and Bangkok and Chiang Mai are the most fruitful places to look for jobs. You can search for openings at schools all over Thailand on wajarn.com, which also features extensive general advice on teaching and living in Thailand. Another useful resource is the excellent wthaivisa.com, whose scores of well-used forums focus on specific topics that range from employment in Thailand to legal issues and cultural and practical topics.

If you're a qualified dive instructor, you might be able to get seasonal work at one of the major resorts – in Phuket, Khao Lak and Ao Nang and on Ko Chang, Ko Phi Phi, Ko Lanta, Ko Samui and Ko Tao, for example. Guesthouse noticeboards occasionally carry adverts for more unusual jobs, such as playing extras in Thai movies. A tourist visa does not entitle you to work in Thailand, so, legally, you'll need to apply for a work permit.

Study, work and volunteer programmes

In addition to the programmes listed below, voluntary opportunities with smaller grassroots projects (see Travel essentials) and wildlife charity projects (see National parks) are available.

AFS Intercultural Programs Australia t02/9215 0077, Canada t1-800/361-7248, NZ t0800/600 300, South Africa t11/447 2673, US t1-800/AFS-INFO; wafs.org. Intercultural exchange organization with programmes in over fifty countries.

Council on International Educational Exchange (CIEE) US t1-207/553-4000, wciee.org. Leading NGO that organizes paid year-long placements as English teachers in schools in Thailand.

Phuket English teachers wphukethasbeengoodtous.org. Welcomes short- and longer-term volunteers to teach and assist on its Practical English Language programme at schools on Phuket. The aim of the foundation is to improve kids' standards of English so that they can get the better-paid jobs in Phuket's tourist industry.

Starfish Ventures wstarfishvolunteers.com. Paying volunteer and gap-year placements in Thailand in the areas of health, childcare, wildlife conservation, community development and teaching.

Volunteer Teaching in Thailand wvolunteerteacherthailand.org. Continuing the good work begun by the thousands of volunteers who came to Khao Lak to help rebuild lives and homes following the 2004 tsunami, this organization teaches English to Khao Lak kids and adults to enhance their future prospects in the local tourist industry. Teaching experience is appreciated but not essential.

Volunthai wvolunthai.com. Invites young volunteers to teach English in rural schools mostly in northeast Thailand. The minimal fees cover homestay accommodation.

Thai language classes The most popular places to study Thai are Chiang Mai and Bangkok, where there's plenty of choice, including private and group lessons for both tourists and expats; note, however, that some schools' main reason for existence is to provide educational visas for long-staying foreigners. The longest-running and best-regarded courses and private lessons are provided by AUA (American University Alumni; wauathailand.org), which has outlets in Bangkok, Pattaya, Rayong and Chiang Mai.

Mail

Overseas airmail usually takes around seven days from Bangkok, a little longer from the more isolated areas (it's worth asking at the post office about their express EMS services, which can cut this down to three days and aren't prohibitively expensive). Post offices in Thailand have recently been quite successfully privatized, and many now offer money-wiring facilities (in association with Western Union), parcel packing, long-distance bus tickets, amulets, whitening cream, you name it. They're generally open Monday to Friday 8.30am to 4.30pm, Saturday 9am to noon; some close Monday to Friday noon to 1pm and may stay open until 6pm, and a few open 9am to noon on Sundays and public holidays. Almost all main post offices across the country operate a poste restante service and will hold letters for one to three months. Mail should be addressed: Name (family name underlined or capitalized), Poste Restante, GPO, Town or City, Thailand. It will be filed by surname, though it's always wise to check under your first initial as well. The smaller post offices pay scant attention to who takes what, but in the busier GPOs you need to show your passport, pay B1 per letter or B2 per parcel received, and sign for them.

Post offices are the best places to buy stamps, though hotels and guesthouses often sell them too, usually charging an extra B1 per stamp. An airmail letter of under 10g costs B17 to send to Europe or Australia and B19 to North America; postcards and aerogrammes cost B15, regardless of where they're going. The surface rate for parcels to the UK is B950 for the first kg, then B175 per kg; to the US B550 for the first kg, then B140 per kg; and to Australia B650 for the first kg, then B110 per kg; the package should reach its destination in three months. The airmail rate for parcels to the UK is B900 for the first kg, then B380 per kg; to the US B950 for the first kg, then B500 per kg; and to Australia B750 for the first kg, then B350 per kg; the package should reach its destination in one or two weeks.

Maps

For most major destinations, the maps in this book should be all you need, though you may want to supplement them with larger-scale maps of Bangkok and the whole country. Bangkok bookshops are the best source of these; where appropriate, detailed local maps and their stockists are recommended throughout the Guide. If you want to buy a map before you get there, Rough Guides' 1:1,200,000 map of Thailand is a good option – and, since it's printed on special rip-proof paper, it won't tear. Reasonable alternatives include the 1:1,500,000 maps produced by Nelles and Bartholomew.

For drivers, the best atlas is Thailand Deluxe Atlas published by thinknet (wthinknet.co.th): at a scale of 1:550,000, it's bilingual and fairly regularly updated, but costs B550. It's available at most bookshops in Thailand where English-language material is sold. They also have a newer Thailand Handy Atlas at 1:1,000,000 for B270, and their mapping is available online at wmapguidethailand.com.

Trekking maps are hard to come by, except in the most popular national parks where you can usually pick up a free handout showing the main trails.

Money and banks

Thailand's unit of currency is the baht (abbreviated to "B"), divided into 100 satang – which are rarely seen these days. Coins come in B1 (silver), B2 (golden), B5 (silver) and B10 (mostly golden, encircled by a silver ring) denominations, notes in B20, B50, B100, B500 and B1000 denominations, inscribed with Western as well as Thai numerals, and generally increasing in size according to value.

At the time of writing, exchange rates were around B30 to US$1, B45 to €1 and B50 to £1. A good site for current exchange rates is wxe.com. Note that Thailand has no black market in foreign currency.

Banking hours are Monday to Friday from 8.30am to 3.30 or 4.30pm, but exchange kiosks in the main tourist centres are always open till at least 5pm, sometimes 10pm, and upmarket hotels change money (at poor rates) 24 hours a day. The Suvarnabhumi Airport exchange counters also operate 24 hours, while exchange kiosks at overseas airports with flights to Thailand usually keep Thai currency.

Sterling and US dollar travellers' cheques are accepted by banks and exchange booths in every sizeable Thai town, and most places also deal in a variety of other currencies; everyone offers better rates for cheques than for straight cash. Generally, a total of B33 in commission and duty is charged per cheque – though kiosks and hotels in isolated places may charge extra – so you'll save money if you deal in larger cheque denominations. Note that Scottish and Northern Irish sterling notes may not be accepted in some places.

American Express, Visa and MasterCard credit and debit cards are accepted at top hotels as well as in some posh restaurants, department stores, tourist shops and travel agents, but surcharging of up to seven percent is rife, and theft and forgery are major industries – try not to let the card out of your sight, always demand any carbon copies, and never leave cards in baggage storage. With a debit or credit card and personal identification number (PIN), you can also withdraw cash from hundreds of 24-hour ATMs around the country. Almost every town now has at least one bank with an ATM that accepts overseas cards (all the banks marked on our maps throughout the Guide have ATMs), and there are a growing number of stand-alone ATMs in supermarkets. However, Thai banks now make a charge of B150 per ATM withdrawal (on top of whatever your bank at home will be charging you); to get around this, go into a bank with your card and passport instead and ask for a cash advance, or check out waeon.co.th, the website of a Japanese bank that operates in Thailand, for locations of their ATMs – they don't charge for ATM withdrawals from foreign bank accounts, though there have been reports of people not receiving cash from Aeon ATMs but having their accounts debited.

Opening hours and public holidays

Most shops open long hours, usually Monday to Saturday from about 8am to 8pm, while department stores operate daily from around 10am to 9pm. Private office hours are generally Monday to Friday 8am to 5pm and Saturday 8am to noon, though in tourist areas these hours are longer, with weekends worked like any other day. Government offices work Monday to Friday 8.30am to noon and 1 to 4.30pm, and national museums tend to stick to these hours too, but some close on Mondays and Tuesdays rather than at weekends. Temples generally open their gates every day from dawn to dusk.

Many tourists only register national holidays because trains and buses suddenly get extraordinarily crowded: although government offices shut on these days, most shops and tourist-oriented businesses carry on regardless, and TAT branches continue to dispense information. (Bank holidays vary slightly from the government office holidays given below: banks close on May 1 and July 1, but not for the Royal Ploughing Ceremony nor for Khao Pansa.) Some national holidays are celebrated with theatrical festivals. The only time an inconvenient number of shops, restaurants and hotels do close is during Chinese New Year, which, though not marked as an official national holiday, brings many businesses to a standstill for several days in late January or February. You'll notice it particularly in the south, where most service industries are Chinese-managed.

Thais use both the Western Gregorian calendar and a Buddhist calendar – the Buddha is said to have died (or entered Nirvana) in the year 543 BC, so Thai dates start from that point: thus 2013 AD becomes 2556 BE (Buddhist Era).

National holidays

Jan 1 Western New Year's Day

Feb (day of full moon) Makha Puja. Commemorates the Buddha preaching to a spontaneously assembled crowd of 1250.

April 6 Chakri Day. The founding of the Chakri dynasty.

April (usually 13–15) Songkhran. Thai New Year.

May 5 Coronation Day

May (early in the month) Royal Ploughing Ceremony. Marks the start of the rice-planting season.

May (day of full moon) Visakha Puja. The holiest of all Buddhist holidays, which celebrates the birth, enlightenment and death of the Buddha.

July (day of full moon) Asanha Puja. The anniversary of the Buddha's first sermon.

July (day after Asanha Puja) Khao Pansa. The start of the annual three-month Buddhist rains retreat, when new monks are ordained.

Aug 12 Queen's birthday and Mothers' Day

Oct 23 Chulalongkorn Day. The anniversary of Rama V's death.

Dec 5 King's birthday and Fathers' Day. Also now celebrated as National Day (instead of Constitution Day).

Dec 10 Constitution Day

Dec 31 Western New Year's Eve

Phones

Most foreign mobile-phone networks have links with Thai networks but you might want to check on roaming rates, which are often exorbitant, before you leave home. To get round this, most travellers purchase a Thai pre-paid SIM card – 1-2-Call (wais.co.th) is the biggest network with the best coverage – for their mobile phone (moe thoe). Available for as little as B50 (sometimes free at airports, for example with True Move) and refillable at 7-Elevens around the country, they offer very cheap calls, both domestically and internationally (especially if you use low-cost international prefixes such as 1-2-Call's "005" or "009"). They also offer very cheap texting and are free of charge for all incoming calls; mobile internet and wi-fi packages are also generally available.

Even cheaper international calls – less than B1/minute to most countries – can be made with a Zay Hi phonecard (wzayhi.com), available in B300 and B500 denominations from post offices and branches of Family Mart. The cheapest option, of course, is to find a guesthouse or café with free wi-fi and Skype from your own device; Skype is also available on the computers in most internet cafés.

When dialling any number in Thailand, you must now always preface it with what used to be the area code, even when dialling from the same area. Where we've given several line numbers – eg t02 431 1802–9 – you can substitute the last digit, 2, with any digit between 3 and 9. For directory enquiries within Thailand, call t1133.

All mobile-phone numbers in Thailand have recently been changed from nine to ten digits, by adding the number "8" after the initial zero (you may still come across cards and brochures giving the old nine-digit number). Note also, however, that Thais tend to change mobile-phone providers – and therefore numbers – comparatively frequently, in search of a better deal.

One final local idiosyncrasy: Thai phone books list people by their first name, not their family name.

Photography

Most towns and all resorts have at least one camera shop where you will be able to get your digital pictures downloaded on to a CD for B100–

150; the shops all have card readers. In tourist centres many internet cafés also offer CD-burning services, though if you want to email your pictures bringing your own cable will make life easier.

Time

Thailand is in the same time zone year-round, with no daylight savings period. It's five hours ahead of South Africa, seven hours ahead of GMT, twelve hours ahead of US Eastern Standard Time, three hours behind Australian Eastern Standard Time and five hours behind New Zealand Standard Time.

Tipping

It is usual to tip hotel bellboys and porters B20–40, and to round up taxi fares to the nearest B10. Most guides, drivers, masseurs, waiters and maids also depend on tips, and although some upmarket hotels and restaurants will add an automatic ten percent service charge to your bill, this is not always shared out.

Tourist information

The Tourism Authority of Thailand, or TAT (wtourismthailand.org), maintains offices in several cities abroad and has dozens of branches within Thailand (all open daily 8.30am–4.30pm, though a few close noon–1pm) plus counters at Suvarnabhumi International Airport. Regional offices should have up-to-date information on local festival dates and perhaps transport schedules, but none of them offers accommodation booking, and service can be variable. You can contact the TAT tourist assistance phoneline from anywhere in the country for free on t1672 (daily 8am–8pm). In Bangkok, the Bangkok Tourism Division is a better source of information on the capital (see Banglamphu). In some smaller towns that don't qualify for a local TAT office, the information gap is filled by a municipal tourist assistance office, though at some of these you may find it hard to locate a fluent English-speaker.

TAT offices abroad

Australia & New Zealand Suite 2002, Level 20, 56 Pitt St, Sydney, NSW 2000 t02/9247 7549, wthailand.net.au.

South Africa Contact the UK office.

UK & Ireland 1st Floor, 17–19 Cockspur St, London SW1Y 5BL t020/7925 2511, einfo@tourismthailand.co.uk.

US & Canada 61 Broadway, Suite 2810, New York, NY 10006 t212/432-0433, einfo@tatny.com; 611 North Larchmont Blvd, 1st Floor, Los Angeles, CA 90004 t323/461-9814, etatla@tat.or.th.

Travellers with disabilities

Thailand makes few provisions for its disabled citizens and this obviously affects travellers with disabilities, but taxis, comfortable hotels and personal tour guides are all more affordable than in the West and most travellers with disabilities find Thais only too happy to offer assistance where they can. Hiring a local tour guide to accompany you on a day's sightseeing is particularly recommended: government tour guides can be arranged through any TAT office.

Most wheelchair-users end up driving on the roads because it's too hard to negotiate the uneven pavements, which are high to allow for flooding and invariably lack dropped kerbs. Crossing the road can be a trial, particularly in Bangkok and other big cities, where it's usually a question of climbing steps up to a bridge rather than taking a ramped underpass. Few buses and trains have ramps but in Bangkok some Skytrain stations and all subway stations have lifts.

Several tour companies in Thailand specialize in organizing trips featuring adapted facilities, accessible transport and escorts. The

Bangkok-based Help and Care Travel Company (t081 375 0792, wwheelchairtours.com) designs accessible holidays in Thailand for slow walkers and wheelchair-users, as well as offering airport transfers and personal assistants. In Chiang Mai, Thai Focus (wthaifocus.com) is used to designing trips for disabled travellers and can provide wheelchair rental. Mermaid's Dive Centre in Pattaya (t038 232219, wlearn-in-asia.com/handicapped_diving.htm) runs International Association of Handicapped Divers programmes for disabled divers and instructors (see Jomtien Beach and Buddha Hill).

When to go

The climate of most of Thailand is governed by three seasons: rainy (roughly May–Oct), caused by the southwest monsoon dumping moisture gathered from the Andaman Sea and the Gulf of Thailand; cool (Nov–Feb); and hot (March–May). The rainy season is the least predictable of the three, and worth considering when thinking about the best time to visit, varying in length and intensity from year to year, but it's never a case of the heavens opening in May and not closing again till October: there'll be rain most days, but often only for a few hours in the afternoon or at night. The rains usually gather force between June and August, coming to a peak in September and October, when unpaved roads are reduced to mud troughs. The cool season is the pleasantest time to visit, although temperatures can still reach a broiling 30°C in the middle of the day. In the hot season, when temperatures often rise to 35°C in Bangkok, the best thing to do is to hit the beach.

Within this scheme, slight variations are found from region to region. The upland, less humid north experiences the greatest range of temperatures: at night in the cool season the thermometer dips markedly, occasionally approaching zero on the higher slopes, and this region is often hotter than the central plains between March and May. It's the northeast that gets the very worst of the hot season, with clouds of dust gathering above the parched fields, and humid air too. In southern Thailand, temperatures are more consistent throughout the year, with less variation the closer you get to the equator. The rainy season hits the Andaman coast of the southern peninsula harder than anywhere else in the country: rainfall can start in April and usually persists until November.

One area of the country, the Gulf coast of the southern peninsula, lies outside this general pattern. With the sea immediately to the east, this coast and its offshore islands feel the effects of the northeast monsoon, which brings rain between October and January, especially in November, but suffers less than the Andaman coast from the southwest monsoon.

Overall, the cool season is the best time to come to Thailand: as well as having more manageable temperatures and less rain, it offers waterfalls in full spate and the best of the upland flowers in bloom. Bear in mind, however, that it's also the busiest season, so forward planning is essential.

Experiences in Thailand

Bangkok

Same same, but different. This Thailish T-shirt philosophy sums up Bangkok, a city where the familiar and the exotic collide like the flavours on a plate of pàt tai.

Full-on Food

Until you've eaten on a Bangkok street, noodles mingling with your sweat amid a cloud of exhaust fumes, you haven't actually eaten Thai food. It can be an intense mix: the base flavours – spicy, sour, sweet and salty – aren't exactly meat and potatoes. But for adventurous foodies who don't need white tablecloths, there's probably no better dining destination in the world. And with immigration bringing every regional Thai and international cuisine to the capital, it's also a truly diverse experience. And perhaps best of all, Bangkok has got to be one of the best-value dining destinations in the world.

Fun Folks

The language barrier can seem huge, but it's never prevented anybody from getting along with the Thai people. The capital's cultural underpinnings are evident in virtually all facets of everyday life, and most enjoyably through its residents' sense of fun (known in Thai as sà·nùk). In Bangkok, anything worth doing should have an element of sà·nùk. Ordering food, changing money and haggling at markets will usually involve a sense of playfulness – a dash of flirtation, perhaps – and a smile. It's a language that doesn't require words, and one that's easy to learn.

Urban Exploration

The Bohemian Blog

With so much of its daily life conducted on the street, there are few cities in the world that reward exploration as handsomely as Bangkok does. Cap off an extended boat trip with a visit to a hidden market. A stroll off Banglamphu's beaten track can lead to a conversation with a monk. Get lost in the tiny lanes of Chinatown and stumble upon a Chinese opera performance. Or after dark, let the BTS (Skytrain) escort you to Sukhumvit, where the local nightlife scene reveals a cosmopolitan and dynamic city.

Contrasts

It's the contradictions that provide the City of Angels with its rich, multifaceted personality. Here, climate-controlled megamalls sit side by side with 200-year-old village homes; gold-spired temples share space with neon-lit strips of sleaze; slow-moving traffic is bypassed by longtail boats plying the royal river; Buddhist monks dressed in robes shop for the latest smartphones; and streets lined with food carts are overlooked by restaurants perched on top of skyscrapers. And as Bangkok races towards the future, these contrasts will never stop supplying the city with its unique and ever-changing strain of Thai-ness.

Experiences in Bangkok

Siam Square, Pratunam, Ploenchit & Ratchathewi

Multistorey malls, outdoor shopping precincts and never-ending markets leave no doubt that Siam Square, Pratunam and Phloen Chit combine to form Bangkok's commercial district. The BTS (Skytrain) interchange at Siam has also made this area the centre of modern Bangkok, while only a few blocks away, scruffy Ratchathewi has a lot more in common with provincial Thai cities.

Jim Thompson House

Top choice historic building in Siam Square, Pratunam, Ploenchit & Ratchathewi

Price - adult/student 150/100B

Hours - 9am-6pm, compulsory tours every 20 min

Contact - http://www.jimthompsonhouse.com

Location - 6 Soi Kasem San 2, Bangkok, Thailand

This jungly compound is the former home of the eponymous American silk entrepreneur and art collector. Born in Delaware in 1906, Thompson briefly served in the Office of Strategic Services (the forerunner of the CIA) in Thailand during WWII. He settled in Bangkok after the war, when his neighbours' handmade silk caught his eye and piqued his business sense; he sent samples to fashion houses in Milan, London and Paris, gradually building a steady worldwide clientele.

In addition to textiles, Thompson also collected parts of various derelict Thai homes and had them reassembled in their current location in 1959. Some of the homes were brought from the old royal capital of Ayuthaya; others were pulled down and floated across the klorng (canal; also spelt khlong) from Baan Khrua, including the first building you enter on the tour. One striking departure from tradition is the way each wall has its exterior side facing the house's interior, thus exposing the wall's bracing system. His small but splendid Asian art collection and his personal belongings are also on display in the main house.

Thompson's story doesn't end with his informal reign as Bangkok's best-adapted foreigner, however. While out for an afternoon walk in the Cameron Highlands of western Malaysia in 1967, Thompson mysteriously disappeared. That same year his sister was murdered in the USA, fuelling various conspiracy theories. Was it communist spies? Business rivals? Or a man-eating tiger? Although the mystery has never been solved, evidence revealed by American journalist Joshua Kurlantzick in his profile of Thompson, The Ideal Man, suggests that the vocal anti-American stance Thompson took later in his life may have made him a potential target of suppression by the CIA.

Beware well-dressed touts in soi near the Thompson house who will tell you it is closed and try to haul you off on a dodgy buying spree.

MBK Center

Top choice shopping centre in Siam Square, Pratunam, Ploenchit & Ratchathewi

Hours - 10am-10pm

Contact - http://www.mbk-center.com

Location - cnr Th Phra Ram I & Th Phayathai, Bangkok, Thailand

This eight-storey market in a mall has emerged as one of Bangkok's top attractions. On any given weekend half of Bangkok's residents (and most of its tourists) can be found here combing through a seemingly inexhaustible range of small stalls, shops and merchandise.

MBK is Bangkok's cheapest place to buy mobile phones and accessories (4th floor). It's also one of the better places to stock up on camera gear (ground floor and 5th floor), and the expansive food court (6th floor) is one of the best in town.

Baan Khrua

Area in Siam Square, Pratunam, Ploenchit & Ratchathewi

This canalside neighbourhood dates back to the turbulent years at the end of the 18th century, when Cham Muslims from Cambodia and Vietnam fought on the side of the new Thai king and were rewarded with this plot of land east of the new capital. The immigrants brought their silk-weaving traditions with them, and the community grew when the residents built Khlong Saen Saeb to better connect them to the river.

The 1950s and '60s were boom years for Baan Khrua after Jim Thompson hired the weavers and began exporting their silks across the globe. The last 50 years, however, haven't been so great. Silk production was moved elsewhere following Thompson's disappearance, and the community spent 15 years successfully fighting to stop a freeway being built right through it. Through all this, many Muslims moved out of the area; today it is estimated that only about 30% of the population is Muslim, the rest primarily immigrants from northeast Thailand.

Today's Baan Khrua consists of old, tightly packed homes threaded by tiny paths barely wide enough for two people to pass. There's a mosque, and two family-run outfits, Phamai Baan Krua and Aood Bankrua Thai Silk, continue to be involved in every step of silk cloth production, from the dyeing of threads to weaving the cloth by hand on old wood looms. Of the two, Phamai Baan Krua claims to be the original. Run by English- and German-speaking Niphon Manuthas, the company continues to produce the type of high-quality handwoven silk that originally attracted Jim Thompson, at much cheaper prices than a certain more famous store across the klorng.

Baan Khrua is an easy stop after visiting Jim Thompson House; simply cross the bridge over the canal at the end of Soi Kasem San 3. Alternatively, from the BTS stop at Ratchathewi, enter Soi Phaya Nak, take the third left (the street that leads to Da-Ru-Fa-Lah Mosque), following it to the canal; turn right and look for the signs.

Erawan Shrine

Monument in Siam Square, Pratunam, Ploenchit & Ratchathewi

Hours - 6am-11pm

Location - cnr Th Ratchadamri & Th Phloen Chit, Bangkok, Thailand

The Erawan Shrine was originally built in 1956 as something of a last-ditch effort to end a string of misfortunes that occurred during the construction of a hotel, at that time known as the Erawan Hotel.

After several incidents ranging from injured construction workers to the sinking of a ship carrying marble for the hotel, a Brahmin priest was consulted. Since the hotel was to be named after the elephant escort of Indra in Hindu mythology, the priest determined that Erawan required a passenger, and suggested it be that of Lord Brahma. A statue was built and, lo and behold, the misfortunes miraculously ended.

Although the original Erawan Hotel was demolished in 1987, the shrine still exists, and today remains an important place of pilgrimage for

Thais, particularly those in need of some material assistance. Those making a wish from the statue should ideally come between 7am and 8am, or 7pm and 8pm, and should offer a specific list of items that includes candles, incense, sugar cane or bananas, all of which are almost exclusively given in multiples of seven. Particularly popular are teak elephants, with money from the sale of these items donated to a charity run by the current hotel, the Grand Hyatt Erawan. And as the tourist brochures depict, it is also possible to charter a classical Thai dance, often done as a way of giving thanks if a wish is granted.

A bomb exploded near the shrine in August 2015, killing 20 and slightly damaging the shrine. It was repaired and reopened just two days later.

Banglamphu

Leafy lanes, antique shophouses, buzzing wet markets and golden temples convene in Banglamphu – easily the city's most quintessentially 'Bangkok' neighbourhood. It's a quaint postcard picture of the city that used to be, that is until you stumble upon Th Khao San, arguably the world's most famous backpacker enclave.

Experiences in Banglamphu

Golden Mount

Buddhist temple in Banglamphu

Price - admission to summit of Golden Mount 10B

Hours - 7.30am-5.30pm

Location - off Th Boriphat, Bangkok, Thailand

Even if you're wát-ed out, you should tackle the brisk ascent to the Golden Mount. Serpentine steps wind through an artificial hill shaded by gnarled trees, some of which are signed in English, and past graves and pictures of wealthy benefactors. At the peak, you'll find a breezy 360-degree view of Bangkok's most photogenic side.

The hill was created when a large stupa, under construction by Rama III (King Phranangklao; r 1824–51), collapsed because the soft soil beneath would not support it. The resulting mud-and-brick hill was left to sprout weeds until Rama IV (King Monkut; r 1851–68) built a small stupa on its crest. Rama V (King Chulalongkorn; r 1868–1910) later added to the structure and housed a Buddha relic from India (given to him by the British government) in the stupa. The concrete walls were added during WWII to prevent the hill from eroding.

In November there's a festival in the grounds that includes an enchanting candlelight procession up the Golden Mount.

Krua Apsorn

Price - mains 100-450B

Hours - 0.30am-8pm Mon-Sat

Contact - http://www.kruaapsorn.com

Location - Th Din So, Bangkok, Thailand

This cafeteria-like dining room is a favourite of members of the Thai royal family and restaurant critics alike. Just about all of the central and southern Thai dishes are tasty, but regulars never miss the chance to order the decadent stir-fried crab with yellow pepper chili or the tortilla Española–like fluffy crab omelette.

There's another branch on Th Samsen in Thewet and Dusit.

Brick Bar

Live music in Banglamphu

Price - admission Sat & Sun 150B

Hours - 7pm-1.30am

Contact - http://www.brickbarkhaosan.com

Location - basement, Buddy Lodge, 265 Th Khao San, Bangkok, Thailand

This basement pub, one of our fave destinations in Bangkok for live music, hosts a nightly revolving cast of bands for an almost exclusively Thai crowd – many of whom will end the night dancing on the tables. Brick Bar can get infamously packed, so be sure to get there early.

Wat Suthat

Top choice buddhist temple in Banglamphu

Price - 20B

Hours - 8.30am-9pm

Location - Th Bamrung Meuang, Bangkok, Thailand

Other than being just plain huge and impressive, Wat Suthat also holds the highest royal temple grade. Inside the wí·hǎhn (sanctuary for a Buddha sculpture) are intricate Jataka (stories of the Buddha) murals and the 8m-high Phra Si Sakayamuni, Thailand's largest surviving Sukhothai-period bronze, cast in the former capital of Sukhothai in the 14th century. Today, the ashes of Rama VIII (King Ananda Mahidol; r 1935–46) are contained in the base of the image.

Behind the wí·hăhn, the bòht (ordination hall) is the largest of its kind in the country. To add to its list of 'largests', Wat Suthat holds the rank of Rachavoramahavihan, the highest royal temple grade. It also maintains a special place in the national religion because of its association with the Brahman priests who perform important ceremonies, such as the Royal Ploughing Ceremony in May. These priests also perform religious rites at two Hindu shrines near the wát – Dhevasathan on Th Din So, and the smaller Vishnu Shrine on Th Unakan.

Northern Bangkok

Once ringed by rice fields, modern Bangkok has since expanded in every possible direction with few concessions to agriculture or charm. Within northern Bangkok, other than some of the city's best markets, sights are relatively few and far between, but the upside is that the area is a good place to get a taste of provincial Thailand if you don't have the time to go upcountry.

Experiences in Northern Bangkok

Chatuchak Weekend Market

Top choice market in Northern Bangkok

Hours - 7am-6pm Wed & Thu (plants only), 6pm-12pm Fri (wholesale only), 9am-6pm Sat & Sun

Contact - http://www.chatuchakmarket.org

Location - 587/10 Th Phahonyothin, Bangkok, Thailand

Among the largest markets in the world, Chatuchak seems to unite everything buyable, from used vintage sneakers to baby squirrels. Plan to spend a full day here, as there's plenty to see, do and buy. But come early, ideally around 10am, to beat the crowds and the heat.

There is an information centre and a bank with ATMs and foreign-exchange booths at the Chatuchak Park Office, near the northern end of the market's Soi 1, Soi 2 and Soi 3. Schematic maps and toilets are located throughout the market.

Friday nights from around 8pm to midnight, several vendors, largely those selling clothing, accessories and food, open up shop in Chatuchak. There are a few vendors on weekday mornings, and a daily vegetable, plant and flower market opposite the market's southern side. One section of the latter, known as the Or Tor Kor Market, sells fantastically gargantuan fruit and seafood, and has a decent food court as well.

Once you're deep in the bowels of Chatuchak, it will seem like there is no order and no escape, but the market is arranged into relatively coherent sections. Use the clock tower as a handy landmark.

Antiques, Handicrafts & Souvenirs

Section 1 is the place to go for Buddha statues, old LPs and other random antiques. More secular arts and crafts, such as musical instruments and hill-tribe items can be found in Sections 25 and 26. Baan Sin Thai sells a mixture of kŏhn masks and old-school Thai toys, all of which make fun souvenirs, and Kitcharoen Dountri specialises in Thai musical instruments, including flutes, whistles, drums and CDs of classical Thai music. Other quirky gifts include the lifelike plastic Thai fruit and vegetables at Marché, or their scaled-down miniature counterparts nearby at Papachu.

184

Clothing & Accessories

Clothing dominates most of Chatuchak, starting in Section 8 and continuing through the even-numbered sections to 24. Sections 5 and 6 deal in used clothing for every Thai youth subculture, from punks to cowboys, while Soi 7, where it transects Sections 12 and 14, is heavy on the more underground hip-hop and skate fashions. Somewhat more sophisticated independent labels can be found in Sections 2 and 3, while tourist-sized clothes and textiles are in Sections 8 and 10.

For accessories, several shops in Sections 24 and 26, such as Orange Karen Silver, specialise in chunky silver jewellery and semiprecious uncut stones.

Eating & Drinking

Lots of Thai-style eating and snacking will stave off Chatuchak rage (cranky behaviour brought on by dehydration or hunger), and numerous food stalls set up shop between Sections 6 and 8. Long-standing standouts include Foontalop, an incredibly popular Isan restaurant; Café Ice, a Western-Thai fusion joint that does good, if overpriced, pàt tai (fried noodles) and tasty fruit shakes; Toh-Plue, which does all the Thai standards; and Saman Islam, a Thai-Muslim restaurant that serves a tasty chicken biryani. Viva 8 features a DJ and, when we stopped by, a chef making huge platters of paella. And as evening draws near, down a beer at Viva's, a cafe-bar that features live music.

Housewares & Decor

The western edge of the market, particularly Sections 8 to 26, specialises in all manner of housewares, from cheap plastic buckets to expensive brass woks. This area is a particularly good place to stock up on inexpensive Thai ceramics, ranging from celadon to the traditional rooster-themed bowls from Lampang.

PL Bronze has a huge variety of stainless-steel flatware, and Ton-Tan deals in coconut- and sugar-palm-derived plates, bowls and other utensils.

Those looking to spice up the house should stop by Spice Boom, were you can find dried herbs and spices for both consumption and decoration. Other notable olfactory indulgences include the handmade soaps, lotions, salts and scrubs at D-narn, and the fragrant perfumes and essential oils at AnyaDharu Scent Library.

For less utilitarian goods, Section 7 is a virtual open-air gallery – we particularly liked Pariwat A-nantachina for Bangkok-themed murals. Several shops in Section 10, including Tuptim Shop, sell new and antique Burmese lacquerware. Meng features a dusty mish-mash of quirky antiques from both Thailand and Myanmar.

Pets

Possibly the most fun you'll ever have window-shopping will be petting puppies and cuddling kittens in Sections 13 and 15. Soi 9 of the former features several shops that deal solely in clothing for pets. It's also worth noting that this section has, in the past, been associated with the sale of illegal wildlife, although much of this trade has been driven underground.

Plants & Gardening

The interior perimeter of Sections 2 to 4 feature a huge variety of potted plants, flowers, herbs, fruits, and the accessories needed to maintain them. Many of these shops are also open on weekday afternoons.

Chang Chui

Market in Northern Bangkok

Price - 20-40B

Hours - 11am-11pm Tue-Sun

Contact - http://www.en.changchuibangkok.com

Location - 460/8 Th Sirindhorn, Bangkok, Thailand

An abandoned airplane, craft-beer bars, a hipster barber shop, performance spaces, a skull-shaped florist, an insect-themed restaurant... This tough-to-pin-down marketplace is one of the most eclectic and exciting openings Bangkok has seen in years. Spanning 18 different structures (all of which are made from discarded objects), a handful of the outlets are open during the day, but the best time to go is during weekend evenings, when the place has the vibe of an artsy, more sophisticated Chatuchak Weekend Market.

Route 66

Club in Northern Bangkok

Price - 300B

Hours - 8pm-2am

Contact - http://www.route66club.com

Location - 29/33-48 RCA/Royal City Ave, Bangkok, Thailand

This vast club has been around just about as long as RCA has, but frequent facelifts and expansions have kept it relevant. Top 40 hip hop rules the main space here, although there are several different themed 'levels', featuring anything from Thai pop to live music.

Nonthaburi Market

Market in Northern Bangkok

Hours - 5-9am

Location - Tha Nam Nonthaburi, Nonthaburi, Bangkok, Thailand

Exotic fruits, towers of dried chillies, smoky grills and the city's few remaining rickshaws form a very un-Bangkok backdrop at this, one of the most expansive and atmospheric produce markets in the area. Come early though, as most vendors are gone by 9am.

To get to the market, take the Chao Phraya Express Boat to Nonthaburi Pier, the northernmost stop for most lines. The market is a two-minute walk east along the main road from the pier.

Ko Ratanakosin & Thonburi

The artificial island of Ko Ratanakosin is Bangkok's birthplace, and the Buddhist temples and royal palaces here comprise some of the city's most important and most visited sights. By contrast, Thonburi, located across Mae Nam Chao Phraya (Chao Phraya River), is a seemingly forgotten yet visit-worthy zone of sleepy residential districts connected by klorng (canals; also spelt khlong).

Experiences in Ko Ratanakosin & Thonburi

Wat Pho

Top choice buddhist temple in Ko Ratanakosin & Thonburi

Price - 100B

Hours - 8.30am-6.30pm

Location - Th Sanam Chai, Bangkok, Thailand

You'll find (slightly) fewer tourists here than at Wat Phra Kaew, but Wat Pho is our fave among Bangkok's biggest sights. In fact, the compound incorporates a host of superlatives: the city's largest reclining Buddha, the largest collection of Buddha images in Thailand and the country's earliest centre for public education.

Almost too big for its shelter is Wat Pho's highlight, the genuinely impressive Reclining Buddha.

The rambling grounds of Wat Pho cover eight hectares, with the major tourist sites occupying the northern side of Th Chetuphon and the monastic facilities found on the southern side. The temple compound is also the national headquarters for the teaching and preservation of traditional Thai medicine, including Thai massage, a mandate legislated by Rama III when the tradition was in danger of extinction. The famous massage school has two massage pavilions located within the temple area and additional rooms within the training facility outside the temple.

Wat Phra Kaew

Top choice buddhist temple in Ko Ratanakosin & Thonburi

Price - 500B

Hours - 8.30am-3.30pm

Location - Th Na Phra Lan, Bangkok, Thailand

Architecturally fantastic, this temple complex is also the spiritual core of Thai Buddhism and the monarchy, symbolically united in what is the country's most holy image, the Emerald Buddha. Attached to the temple complex is the Grand Palace, the former royal residence, once a sealed city of intricate ritual and social stratification.

The ground was consecrated in 1782, the first year of Bangkok rule, and is today Bangkok's biggest tourist attraction and a pilgrimage destination for devout Buddhists and nationalists. The 94.5-hectare grounds encompass more than 100 buildings that represent 200 years of royal history and architectural experimentation. Most of the architecture, royal or sacred, can be classified as Ratanakosin (old-Bangkok style).

Emerald Buddha

Upon entering Wat Phra Kaew you'll meet the yaksha, brawny guardian giants from the Ramakian. Beyond them is a courtyard where the central bòht (ordination hall) houses the Emerald Buddha. The spectacular ornamentation inside and out does an excellent job of distracting first-time visitors from paying their respects to the image. Here's why: the Emerald Buddha is only 66cm tall and sits so high above worshippers in the main temple building that the gilded shrine is more striking than the small figure it cradles. No one knows exactly where it comes from or who sculpted it, but it first appeared on record in 15th-century Chiang Rai in northern Thailand. Stylistically it seems to belong to Thai artistic periods of the 13th to 14th centuries.

Because of its royal status, the Emerald Buddha is ceremoniously draped in monastic robes. There are now three royal robes: for the hot, rainy and cool seasons. The three robes are still solemnly changed by the king at the beginning of each season.

Ramakian Murals

Outside the main bòht is a stone statue of the Chinese goddess of mercy, Kuan Im, and nearby are two cow figures, representing the year of Rama I's birth. In the 2km-long cloister that defines the perimeter of the complex are 178 murals depicting the Ramakian (the Thai version of the

Indian Ramayana epic) in its entirety, beginning at the north gate and moving clockwise around the compound.

The story begins with the hero, Rama (the greenfaced character), and his bride, Sita (the beautiful topless maiden). The young couple are banished to the forest, along with Rama's brother. In this pastoral setting, the evil king Ravana (the character with many arms and faces) disguises himself as a hermit in order to kidnap Sita.

Rama joins forces with Hanuman, the monkey king (logically depicted as the white monkey), to attack Ravana and rescue Sita. Although Rama has the pedigree, Hanuman is the unsung hero. He is loyal, fierce and clever. En route to the final fairy-tale ending, great battles and schemes of trickery ensue until Ravana is finally killed. After withstanding a loyalty test of fire, Sita and Rama are triumphantly reunited.

If the temple grounds seem overrun by tourists, the mural area is usually mercifully quiet and shady.

Wat Arun

Top choice buddhist temple in Ko Ratanakosin & Thonburi

Price - 50B

Hours - 8am-6pm

Contact - http://www.watarun.net

Location - off Th Arun Amarin, Bangkok, Thailand

After the fall of Ayuthaya, King Taksin ceremoniously clinched control here on the site of a local shrine and established a royal palace and a temple to house the Emerald Buddha. The temple was renamed after the Indian god of dawn (Aruna) and in honour of the literal and symbolic founding of a new Ayuthaya. Today it is one of Bangkok's most iconic structures – not to mention one of the few Buddhist temples one is encouraged to climb on.

It wasn't until the capital and the Emerald Buddha were moved to Bangkok that Wat Arun received its most prominent characteristic: the

82m-high þrahng (Khmer-style tower). The tower's construction was started during the first half of the 19th century by Rama II (King Phraphutthaloetla Naphalai; r 1809–24) and later completed by Rama III (King Phranangklao; r 1824–51). Steep stairs lead to the top, from where there's amazing views of Mae Nam Chao Phraya. Not apparent from a distance are the ornate floral mosaics made from broken, multihued Chinese porcelain, a common temple ornamentation in the early Ratanakosin period, when Chinese ships calling at the port of Bangkok discarded tonnes of old porcelain as ballast.

Also worth an inspection is the interior of the bòht (ordination hall). The main Buddha image is said to have been designed by Rama II himself. The murals date from the reign of Rama V (King Chulalongkorn; r 1868–1910); particularly impressive is one that depicts Prince Siddhartha encountering examples of birth, old age, sickness and death outside his palace walls, an experience that led him to abandon the worldly life. The ashes of Rama II are interred in the base of the presiding Buddha image.

Frequent cross-river ferries run over to Wat Arun from Tien Pier (3B).

Amulet Market

Market in Ko Ratanakosin & Thonburi

Hours - 7am-5pm

Location - Th Maha Rat, Bangkok, Thailand

This arcane and fascinating market claims both the footpaths along Th Maha Rat and Th Phra Chan, as well as a dense network of covered market stalls that run south from Phra Chan Pier; the easiest entry point is clearly marked Trok Maha That. The trade is based around small talismans carefully prized by collectors, monks, taxi drivers and people in dangerous professions.

Potential buyers, often already sporting many amulets, can be seen bargaining and flipping through magazines dedicated to the amulets, some of which command astronomical prices. It's a great place to just wander and watch men (because it's rarely women) looking through magnifying glasses at the tiny amulets, seeking hidden meaning and, if they're lucky, hidden value.

Riverside, Silom & Lumphini

Although you may not see it behind the office blocks, high-rise condos and hotels, Mae Nam Chao Phraya forms a watery backdrop to these linked neighbourhoods. History is still palpable in the riverside area's crumbling architecture, while heading inland, Silom, Bangkok's de facto financial district, is frenetic and modern, Th Sathon is the much more subdued embassy zone and Lumphini is dominated by central Bangkok's largest green zone.

Experiences in Riverside, Silom & Lumphini

Nahm

Thai in Riverside, Silom & Lumphini

Price - set lunch 600-1600B, set dinner 2500B, mains 310-800B

Hours - noon-2pm Mon-Fri, 7-10.30pm daily

Contact - http://www.comohotels.com/metropolitanbangkok/dining/nahm,

02 625 3388

Location - ground fl, Metropolitan Hotel, 27 Th Sathon Tai/South, Bangkok, Thailand

Australian chef-author David Thompson is the man behind one of Bangkok's – and if you believe the critics, the world's – best Thai restaurants. Using ancient cookbooks as his inspiration, Thompson has given new life to previously extinct dishes with exotic descriptions such as 'smoked fish curry with prawns, chicken livers, cockles, chillies and black pepper'.

Dinner is best approached via the multicourse set meal, while lunch means kà·nŏm jeen, thin rice noodles served with curries.

If you're expecting bland, gentrified Thai food meant for foreigners, prepare to be disappointed. Reservations essential.

Moon Bar

Bar in Riverside, Silom & Lumphini

Hours - 5pm-1am

Contact - http://www.banyantree.com/en/web/banyantree/ap-thailand-bangkok/vertigo-and-moon-bar

Location - 61st fl, Banyan Tree Hotel, 21/100 Th Sathon Tai/South, Bangkok, Thailand

An alarmingly short barrier at this rooftop bar is all that separates patrons from the street, 61 floors down. Located on top of the Banyan Tree Hotel, Moon Bar claims to be among the highest alfresco bars in the world. It's also a great place from which to see the Phrapradaeng Peninsula, a vast green area that's colloquially known as Bangkok's green lung.

Save your shorts and sandals for another locale.

Lumpini Park

Park in Riverside, Silom & Lumphini

Hours - 4.30am-9pm

Location - bounded by Th Sarasin, Th Phra Ram IV, Th, Witthayu/Wireless Rd & Th Ratchadamri, Bangkok, Thailand

Named after the Buddha's place of birth in Nepal, Lumphini Park is the best way to escape Bangkok without actually leaving town. Shady paths, a large artificial lake and swept lawns temporarily blot out the roaring traffic and hulking concrete towers.

There are paddleboats for lovers, playgrounds for the kids and enormous monitor lizards for the whole family. One of the best times to visit the park is before 7am, when the air is fresh (well, relatively so for Bangkok) and legions of Thai-Chinese are practising t'ai chi. The park reawakens with the evening's cooler temperatures – aerobics classes collectively sweat to a techno soundtrack. Late at night the borders of the park are frequented by streetwalking prostitutes, both male and female.

Chaophraya Cruise

Boating in Riverside, Silom & Lumphini

Price - 1700B

Hours - cruise 7-9pm

Contact - http://www.chaophrayacruise.com, 02 541 5599

Location - Bangkok, Thailand

Dinner cruise along Mae Nam Chao Phraya.

Chinatown

Although many generations removed from the motherland, Bangkok's Chinatown could be a bosom buddy of any Chinese city. The streets are crammed with bird's-nest restaurants, gaudy gold and jade shops, and flashing neon signs in Chinese characters. It's Bangkok's most hectic neighbourhood, where half the fun is getting completely lost.

Experiences in Chinatown

Nay Hong

Street food in Chinatown

Price - mains 35-50B

Hours - 4-10pm

Location - off Th Yukol 2, Bangkok, Thailand

The reward for locating this hole-in-the-wall is one of Bangkok's best fried noodle dishes – gŏo·ay đĕe·o kôo·a gài – flat rice noodles fried with garlic oil, chicken and egg. No English-language menu.

To find it, proceed north from the corner of Th Suapa and Th Luang, then turn right into the first side-street; it's at the end of the narrow alleyway.

Wat Traimit (Golden Buddha)

Top choice buddhist temple in Chinatown

Price - 100B

Hours - 8am-5pm

Location - Th Mittaphap Thai-China, Bangkok, Thailand

The attraction at Wat Traimit is undoubtedly the impressive 3m-tall, 5.5-tonne, solid-gold Buddha image, which gleams like, well, gold. Sculpted in the graceful Sukhothai style, the image was 'discovered' some 40 years ago beneath a stucco/plaster exterior, when it fell from a crane while being moved to a new building within the temple compound.

It has been theorised that the covering was added to protect it from marauding hordes, either during the late Sukhothai period or later in the Ayuthaya period when the city was under siege by the Burmese. The temple itself is said to date from the early 13th century.

Donations and a constant flow of tourists have proven profitable, and the statue is now housed in an imposing four-storey marble structure. The 2nd floor of the building is home to the Phra Buddha Maha Suwanna Patimakorn Exhibition, which has exhibits on how the statue was made, discovered and came to arrive at its current home, while the 3rd floor is home to the Yaowarat Chinatown Heritage Center, a small but engaging museum with multimedia exhibits on the history of Bangkok's Chinatown and its residents.

Talat Mai

Market in Chinatown

Hours - 6am-6pm

Location - Soi Yaowarat 6/Charoen Krung 16, Bangkok, Thailand

With nearly two centuries of commerce under its belt, New Market is no longer an entirely accurate name for this strip of commerce. Regardless, this is Bangkok's, if not Thailand's, most Chinese market, and the dried goods, seasonings, spices and sauces will be familiar to anyone who's ever spent time in China. Even if you're not interested in food, the hectic atmosphere (be on guard for motorcycles squeezing between shoppers) and exotic sights and smells culminate in something of a surreal sensory experience.

While much of the market centres on cooking ingredients, the section north of Th Charoen Krung (equivalent to Soi 21, Th Charoen Krung) is known for selling incense, paper effigies and ceremonial sweets – the essential elements of a traditional Chinese funeral.

Talat Noi

Area in Chinatown

Hours - 7am-7pm

Location - off Th Charoen Krung, Bangkok, Thailand

This microcosm of soi life is named after a small (nóy) market (đà·làht) that sets up between Soi 22 and Soi 20, off Th Charoen Krung. Wandering here you'll find streamlike soi turning in on themselves, weaving through noodle shops, grease-stained machine shops and people's living rooms.

Phahurat

Area in Chinatown

Hours - 9am-5pm

Location - Th Chakkaraphet, Bangkok, Thailand

Heaps of South Asian traders set up shop in Bangkok's small but bustling Little India, where everything from Bollywood movies to bindis is sold by enthusiastic, small-time traders. It's a great area to just wander through, stopping for masala chai and a Punjabi sweet as you go.

The bulk of the action unfolds along unmarked Soi ATM, which runs alongside the large India Emporium shopping centre.

The emphasis is on cloth, and Phahurat proffers boisterously coloured textiles, traditional Thai dance costumes, tiaras, sequins, wigs and other accessories to make you look like a cross-dresser, a mŏr lam (Thai country music) performer, or both. Amid the spectacle of colour there are also good deals on machine-made Thai textiles and children's clothes.

Chiang Mai

The former seat of the Lanna kingdom is a blissfully calm and laid-back place to relax and recharge your batteries. Yes you'll be surrounded by other wide-eyed travellers but that scarcely takes away from the fabulous food and leisurely wandering. Participate in a vast array of activities on offer, or just stroll around the backstreets, and discover a city that is still firmly Thai in its atmosphere, and attitude.

A sprawling modern city has grown up around ancient Chiang Mai (เชียงใหม่), ringed by a tangle of superhighways. Despite this, the historic centre of Chiang Mai still feels overwhelmingly residential, more like a sleepy country town than a bustling capital. If you drive in a straight line in any direction, you'll soon find yourself in the lush green countryside and pristine rainforests dotted with churning waterfalls, serene wát, and peaceful country villages – as well as a host of markets and elephant sanctuaries.

Experiences in Chiang Mai

Wat Phra That Doi Suthep

Price - 30B

Hours - 6am-6pm

Location - Th Huay Kaew, Doi Suthep, Chiang Mai, Thailand

Overlooking the city from its mountain throne, Wat Phra That Doi Suthep is one of northern Thailand's most sacred temples, and its founding legend is learned by every schoolkid in Chiang Mai. The wát is a beautiful example of northern Thai architecture, reached via a 306-step staircase flanked by naga (serpents); the climb is intended to help devotees accrue Buddhist merit.

The monastery was established in 1383 by King Keu Naone to enshrine a piece of bone said to be from the shoulder of the historical Buddha.

The bone shard was brought to Lanna by a wandering monk from Sukhothai and it broke into two pieces at the base of the mountain, with one piece being enshrined at Wat Suan Dok. The second fragment was mounted onto a sacred white elephant that wandered the jungle until it died, in the process selecting the spot where the monastery was later founded.

The terrace at the top of the steps is dotted with breadfruit trees, small shrines, rock gardens and monuments, including a statue of the white elephant that carried the Buddha relic to its current resting place. Before entering the inner courtyard, children pay their respects to a lizard-like guardian dragon statue known as 'Mom'.

Steps lead up to the inner terrace, where a walkway circumnavigates the gleaming golden chedi enshrining the relic. The crowning five-tiered umbrella marks the city's independence from Burma and its union with Thailand. Pilgrims queue to leave lotus blossoms and other offerings at the shrines surrounding the chedi, which are studded with Buddha statues in an amazing variety of poses and materials.

Within the monastery compound, the Doi Suthep Vipassana Meditation Center conducts a variety of religious outreach programs for visitors.

Rót daang run to the bottom of the steps to the temple from several points in Chiang Mai, including from in front of the zoo (40B per passenger) and in front of Wat Phra Singh (50B per passenger), but they only leave when they have enough passengers. A charter ride from the centre will cost 300B, or 500B return. Many people cycle up on mountain-biking tours from Chiang Mai, and you can also walk from the university.

Wat Phra Singh

Price - 20B

Hours - 5am-8.30pm

Location - Th Singharat, Chiang Mai, Thailand

Chiang Mai's most revered temple, Wat Phra Singh is dominated by an enormous, mosaic-inlaid wí·hăhn (sanctuary). Its prosperity is plain to see from the lavish monastic buildings and immaculately trimmed grounds, dotted with coffee stands and massage pavilions. Pilgrims flock here to venerate the famous Buddha image known as Phra Singh (Lion Buddha), housed in Wihan Lai Kham, a small chapel immediately south of the chedi to the rear of the temple grounds.

This elegant idol is said to have come to Thailand from Sri Lanka and was enshrined in 1367, and the chapel is similarly striking, with gilded naga (serpent) gables and sumptuous lai·krahm (gold-pattern stencilling) inside.

Despite Phra Singh's exalted status, very little is known about the Phra Singh image, which has more in common with images from northern Thailand than with Buddha statues from Sri Lanka. Adding to the mystery, there are two nearly identical images elsewhere in Thailand, one in the Bangkok National Museum and one in Wat Phra Mahathat Woramahawihan in Nakhon Si Thammarat. Regardless of its provenance, the statue has become a focal point for religious celebrations during the Songkran festival.

As you wander the monastery grounds, note the raised temple library, housed in a dainty teak and stucco pavilion known as Ho Trai, decorated with bas-relief angels in the style of Wat Jet Yot. The temple's main chedi, rising over a classic Lanna-style octagonal base, was constructed by King Pa Yo in 1345; it's often wrapped in bolts of orange cloth by devotees.

Saturday Walking Street

Hours - 4pm-midnight Sat

Location - Th Wualai, Chiang Mai, Thailand

The Saturday Walking Street takes over Th Wualai, running southwest from Pratu Chiang Mai at the southern entrance to the old city. There is barely space to move as locals and tourists from across the world haggle vigorously for carved soaps, novelty dog collars, woodcarvings, Buddha paintings, hill-tribe trinkets, Thai musical instruments, T-shirts, paper lanterns and umbrellas, silver jewellery and herbal remedies.

Talat Pratu Chiang Mai

Price - mains from 40B

Hours - 4am-noon & 6pm-midnight

Location - Th Bamrungburi, Chiang Mai, Thailand

In the early morning, this market is Chiang Mai's larder, selling foodstuffs and ready-made dishes. If you want to make merit to the monks, come early and find the woman who sells pre-assembled food donations (20B); she'll explain the ritual to you. Things quieten by lunchtime, but the burners are re-ignited for a popular night market that sets up along the road.

Riverside Bar & Restaurant

Price - mains 100-370B

Hours - 10am-1am

Location - Th Charoenrat, Chiang Mai, Thailand

Almost everyone ends up at Riverside at some point in their Chiang Mai stay. Set in an old teak house, it feels like a boondocks reimagining of a Hard Rock Cafe, and bands play nightly until late. Stake out a claim on the riverside terrace or the upstairs balcony to catch the evening breezes on the Mae Ping river.

Lanna Folklife Museum

Top choice museum in Chiang Mai

Price - adult/child 90/40B

Hours - 8.30am-5pm Tue-Sun

Location - Th Phra Pokklao, Chiang Mai, Thailand

Set inside the Thai-colonial-style former Provincial Court, dating from 1935, this imaginative museum re-creates Lanna village life in a series of life-size dioramas that explain everything from lai·krahm pottery stencilling and fon lep (a mystical Lanna dance featuring long metal fingernails) to the intricate symbolism of different elements of Lanna-style monasteries.

This is the best first stop before heading to the many wát dotted around the old city.

Wat U Mong

Buddhist temple in Chiang Mai

Price - donations appreciated

Hours - daylight hours

Location - Soi Wat U Mong, Th Khlong Chonprathan, Chiang Mai, Thailand

Not to be confused with the small Wat U Mong in the old city, this historic forest wát is famed for its sylvan setting and its ancient chedi, above a brick platform wormholed with passageways, built around 1380 for the 'mad' monk Thera Jan. As you wander the arched tunnels, you can see traces of the original murals and several venerated Buddha images.

The scrub forest around the platform is scattered with centuries' worth of broken Buddha images. The attendant monks raise cows, deer, chickens and, curiously, English bull terriers, and in the grounds is a pretty artificial lake, surrounded by gù·đì (monastic cottages). Check out the emaciated black-stone Buddha in the Burmese style, behind the chedi.

Wat U Mong is 600m south of Th Suthep near Chiang Mai University; be sure to ask the driver to take you to 'Wat U Mong Thera Jan' so you end up at the right monastery. If coming with your own transport, look for signs to Srithana Resort on Th Suthep.

Railay

Krabi's fairytale limestone formations come to a dramatic climax at Railay (also spelt Rai Leh), the ultimate Andaman gym for rock-climbing fanatics. Monkeys gamble alongside climbers on the gorgeous crags, while down below some of the prettiest beaches in all Thailand are backed by proper jungle.

Accessible only by boat, but just a 15 minute ride from Ao Nang, the busiest parts of Railay are sandwiched between the scrappy, not good for swimming, beach of Hat Railay East and the high-end resorts and beautiful white sand of Hat Railay West and Hat Tham Phra Nang.

Railay is more crowded than it once was and sees many day trippers. Thankfully, though, it remains much less-developed than Ko Phi-Phi and if you head away from Hat Railay West and Hat Railay East, then the resorts disappear and the atmosphere is one of delightfully laidback Thai-Rasta bliss.

Chiang Rai Province

Chiang Rai Province (จังหวัดเชียงราย), Thailand's northernmost province, has a bit of everything: the mountains in the far east are among the most dramatic in the country, the lowland Mekong River floodplains to the northeast are not unlike those one would find much further south in Isan, and the province shares borders with Myanmar and Laos. In terms of people, it's also among Thailand's most ethnically diverse provinces and is home to a significant minority of hill tribes, Shan and other Tai groups, and more recent Chinese immigrants.

Sights in Chiang Rai Province

Mae Fah Luang Art & Culture Park

Top choice museum in Chiang Rai

Price - adult/child 200B/free

Hours - 8.30am - 4.30pm Tue-Sun

Contact - http://www.maefahluang.org/rmfl

Location - 313 Mu 7, Ban Pa Ngiw, Chiang Rai, Thailand

In addition to a museum that houses one of Thailand's biggest collections of Lanna artifacts, this vast, meticulously landscaped compound includes antique and contemporary art, Buddhist temples and other structures.

It's located about 4km west of the centre of Chiang Rai; a túk-túk or taxi here will run around 100B.

Haw Kaew, the park's museum, has a permanent collection of mostly teak-based artifacts and art from across the former Lanna region, as well as a temporary exhibition room.

Haw Kham, a temple-like tower built in 1984 from the remains of 32 wooden houses, is arguably the park's centrepiece. The immense size of the structure – allegedly influenced by Lanna-era Wat Pongsanuk in Lampang – with its Buddha image seemingly hovering over white sand (the latter imported from Ko Samet) and its sacred, candle-lit aura culminate in a vibe not unlike the place of worship of an indigenous cult.

You'll probably have to ask staff to open up Haw Kham Noi, a structure housing folksy but beautiful Buddhist murals taken from a dismantled teak temple in Phrae.

Wat Rong Khun

Top choice buddhist temple in Chiang Rai Province

Hours - 8am-5pm Mon-Fri, to 5.30pm Sat & Sun

Location - off Rte 1/AH2, Chiang Rai Province, Thailand

Whereas most of Thailand's Buddhist temples have centuries of history, Wat Rong Khun's construction began in 1997 by noted Thai painter-turned-architect Chalermchai Kositpipat. Seen from a distance, the temple appears to be made of glittering porcelain; a closer look reveals that the appearance is due to a combination of whitewash and clear-mirrored chips.

It's located about 13km south of Chiang Rai. To get here, hop on one of the regular buses that run from Chiang Rai to Wiang Pa Pao (20B, hourly from 6.15am to 6.10pm).

To enter the temple, you must walk over a bridge and pool of reaching arms (symbolising desire), where inside, instead of the traditional

Buddha life depictions, the artist has painted contemporary scenes representing samsara (the realm of rebirth and delusion). Images such as a plane smashing into the Twin Towers and, oddly enough, Keanu Reeves as Neo from The Matrix (not to mention Elvis, Hello Kitty and Superman, among others), dominate the one finished wall of this work in progress.

The temple suffered minor damage in an earthquake in 2014.

Baandam

Top choice museum in Chiang Rai Province

Price - adult/child 80B/free

Hours - 9am-5pm

Location - off Rte 1/AH2, Chiang Rai Province, Thailand

The bizarre brainchild of Thai National Artist Thawan Duchanee, and a rather sinister counterpoint to Wat Rong Khun, Baandam unites several structures, most of which are stained black and ominously decked out with animal pelts and bones.

It's located 13km north of Chiang Rai in Nang Lae; any Mae Sai–bound bus will drop you off here for around 20B.

The centrepiece is a black, cavernous, temple-like building holding a long wooden dining table and chairs made from deer antlers – a virtual Satan's dining room. Other buildings include white, breast-shaped bedrooms, dark phallus-decked bathrooms, and a bone- and fur-lined 'chapel'. The structures have undeniably discernible northern Thai influences, but the dark tones, flagrant flourishes and all those dead animals coalesce in a way that is more fantasy than reality.

Ayutthaya

Enigmatic temple ruins are strewn across Ayuthaya (อยุธยา), whispering of its glory days as a royal capital. Once replete with gilded temples and treasure-laden palaces, the city was the capital of Siam from 1350 until 1767, when the city was brutally sacked by the Burmese. Only ruins remain from this period of thriving trade and art, but dozens of crumbling temples evoke Ayuthaya's past grandeur. Standing among towering stupas, it's easy to imagine how they looked in their prime.

A day trip is enough to tour temple ruins and catch the flavour of Ayuthaya's faded majesty. But linger for a couple of days and you'll fully experience its otherworldly atmosphere of sloshing riverboats, temple silhouettes drawn sharp against the setting sun, and ruins illuminated at night.

Sights in Ayuthaya

Wat Ratchaburana

Top choice ruins in Ayuthaya

Price - admission 50B

Hours - 8am-6pm

Location - off Th Naresuan, Ayuthaya, Thailand

The prang (Khmer-style stupa) in this sprawling temple complex is one of the best extant versions in the city, with detailed carvings of lotus flowers and mythical creatures; it's surrounded by another four stupas. If you aren't afraid of heights, small spaces or bats, you can climb inside the prang to visit the crypt (the largest in Thailand), decorated with faint murals of the Buddha from the early Ayuthaya period.

The temple was founded in 1424 by King Borom Rachathirat II on the cremation site for his two brothers who died while fighting each other for the throne.

The crypt's gold treasures were famously looted in 1957. The thieves were tracked down, though it was too late for the priceless artefacts, most of which had been melted down and sold on. The remainder of Wat Ratchaburana's gold artefacts are on display in Chao Sam Phraya National Museum.

You can visit Wat Ratchaburana with the 220B multi-temple ticket.

Wat Phra Si Sanphet

Top choice ruins in Ayuthaya

Price - admission 50B

Hours - 8am-6pm

Location - Ayuthaya, Thailand

At this captivating ruined temple, three wonderfully intact stupas form one of Ayuthaya's most iconic views; unlike at many other ruins, it's possible to clamber up the stairs for a lofty vantage point (and epic selfie). Built in the late 15th century, this was a royal temple inside palace grounds; these were the model for Bangkok's Wat Phra Kaew and Royal Palace. This temple once contained a 16m-high standing Buddha (Phra Si Sanphet) covered with at least 143kg of gold.

The gold from the statue was melted down by Burmese conquerors.

A trove of Buddha statues discovered here are now displayed in Bangkok, while wooden door panels from the stupa can be viewed locally at the Chao Sam Phraya National Museum.

You can visit Wat Phra Si Sanphet using Ayuthaya's 220B multi-temple ticket. It's south of the Old Royal Palace.

Wat Mahathat

Ruins in Ayuthaya

Price - admission 50B

Hours - 8am-6.30pm

Location - Th Chee Kun, Ayuthaya, Thailand

Ayuthaya's most photographed attraction is in these temple grounds: a sandstone Buddha head tangled within a bodhi tree's entwined roots. Founded in 1374, during the reign of King Borom Rachathirat I, Wat Mahathat was the seat of the supreme patriarch and the kingdom's most important temple. The central prang (Hindi/Khmer-style stupa) once stood 43m high and it collapsed on its own long before the Burmese sacked the city. It was rebuilt in more recent times, but collapsed again in 1911.

As one of Ayuthaya's most popular tourist attractions, the site can get crowded but the grounds are large; wander a short distance and you can find pockets of calm.

Wat Mahathat can be visited on the 220B multi-temple ticket.

Kanchanaburi

Beyond its hectic modern centre and river views, Kanchanaburi (กาญจนบุรี) has a dark history, paid tribute to at excellent memorials and museums.

During WWII, Japanese forces used Allied prisoners of war (POWs) and conscripted Asian labourers to build a rail route between Thailand and Myanmar. The harrowing story became famous after the publication of Pierre Boulle's book The Bridge Over the River Kwai, based loosely on real events, and the 1957 movie that followed. War cemeteries, museums and the chance to ride a section of the so-called 'Death Railway' draw numerous visitors to Kanchanaburi. Interest in the railway has been reignited by Richard Flanagan's Man Booker Prize-winning novel The Narrow Road to the Deep North (2013), inspired by the experiences of Flanagan's father as a POW.

Kanchanaburi is also an ideal gateway to national parks in Thailand's wild west, and home to an array of lush riverside resorts.

Sights in Kanchanaburi

Death Railway Bridge

Top choice historic site in Kanchanaburi

This 300m-long bridge is heavy with the history of the Thailand–Burma Railway, the construction of which cost thousands of imprisoned labourers their lives. Its centre was destroyed by Allied bombs in 1945; only the outer curved spans are original. You're free to roam over the bridge; stand in a safety point if a train appears. Food and souvenir hawkers surround the bridge, so the site can have a jarring, funfair-like atmosphere; come early or late to avoid the scrum.

The three old trains in the park near the station were used during WWII. Across the river, pop in to the Chinese temple on the right and view the bridge from its tranquil garden. Nothing remains of a second (wooden) bridge the Japanese built 100m downstream.

During the last weekend of November and first weekend of December, an informative sound and light show tells the history of the Death Railway.

Thailand–Burma Railway Centre

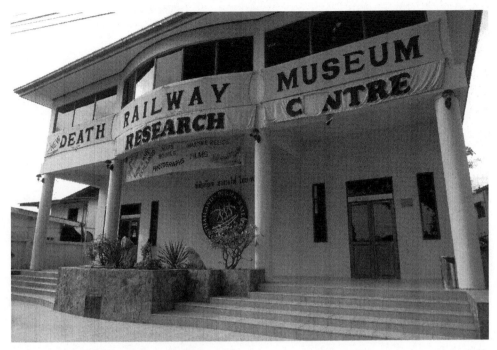

Top choice museum in Kanchanaburi

Price - adult/child 140/60B

Hours - 9am-5pm

Contact - http://www.tbrconline.com, 034 512721

Location - 73 Th Jaokannun, Kanchanaburi, Thailand

This excellent museum balances statistics and historical context with personal accounts of the conditions endured by POWs and other imprisoned labourers forced to build the Thailand–Burma Railway. Kanchanaburi's role in WWII is thoroughly explained, but most of the museum traces the journey of railway workers from transport in cramped boxcars to disease-ridden labour camps in the jungle, as well as survivors' fates after the war. Allow time for the poignant video with testimony from both POWs and Japanese soldiers.

Galleries upstairs display wartime artefacts, and there's a 3m-deep diorama showing how Hellfire Pass got its name. Allow at least an hour for your visit.

For in-depth wartime and railway history, the centre can organise half-day to week-long tours in and around Kanchanaburi; enquire via their website (under 'Railway Pilgrimages').

Wat Tham Seua

Buddhist temple in Kanchanaburi

The centrepiece of this hilltop temple is a striking 18m-high Buddha covered in golden mosaics. One of the merit-making ceremonies for devotees is to place coins in small trays on a conveyor belt that drops donations into a central bowl with a resounding clang. It's fun to ride the steep cable car (per person 20B) to the top of the temple, but you can also climb the stairs.

Surrounding the main Buddha image are several styles of stupa. The biggest, nine stories (69m) high, is full of murals – mostly war related – of Kanchanaburi's history, and Buddha images, including many in seldom-seen postures. The namesake Tiger Cave, flanked by brightly painted tiger statues, is at the base of the hill, to the right of the cable car. The Chinese-style temple next door is Wat Tham Khao Noi, which is more interesting outside than in.

Wat Tham Seua is 12km southeast of central Kanchanaburi. After crossing the city's southernmost bridge, make the first left and follow the river. There's no public transport.

Similan Islands Marine National Park

Known to divers the world over, the beautiful 70-sq-km Similan Islands Marine National Park lies 70km offshore from Phang-Nga Province. Its smooth granite islands are as impressive above the bright-aqua water as below, topped with rainforest, edged with blindingly white beaches and fringed by coral reefs. Coral bleaching has killed off many hard corals, but soft corals are still intact and the fauna and fish are still there. However, the Similans are now on the tourist trail and many beaches and snorkel sites get packed out with day trippers.

You can stay on Ko Miang (Island 4) and Ko Similan. The park visitors centre and most facilities are on Ko Miang. The islands all have names, but are more commonly known by their numbers.

Hat Khao Lak is the park's jumping-off point. The pier and mainland national park headquarters are at Thap Lamu, 12km south (Hwy 4, then Rte 4147).

Sights in Similan Islands Marine National Park

Ko Tachai

Island in Similan Islands Marine National Park

Twin Peaks at Ko Tachai is one of the best dive sites in the Similans, although strong currents mean it is generally reserved for experienced divers. Expect to see big fish: Manta Rays and Leopard sharks, as well as turtles.

Ko Tachai, along with Ko Bon, became part of the national park in 1998, when the park was expanded from its original nine islands.

Ko Bon

Island in Similan Islands Marine National Park

In 1998, the park was expanded from its original nine islands to include uninhabited Ko Bon and Ko Tachai. The west ridge of Ko Bon is the number one place in Thailand to see Manta Rays, because the coral remains in fine condition and so attracts many fish. Currents here can be strong, so it is often reserved for experienced divers.

Hin Pousar

Dive site in Similan Islands Marine National Park

Named because the rocky outcrops here are said to resemble an elephant's head, the strong currents mean this site is for advanced divers. There are dive-throughs and marine life ranging from tiny plume worms and soft corals to schooling fish, octopus and reef sharks.

Pai

Spend enough time in northern Thailand and eventually you'll hear the comparisons between Pai (ปาย) and Bangkok's Khao San Rd. Although the comparisons are definitely a stretch, over the last decade the small town has started to resemble something of a Thai island getaway – without the beaches. Guesthouses appear to outnumber private residences in the 'downtown' area, a trekking agency or restaurant is never more than a few steps away and the nights buzz with the sound of live music and partying.

Despite all this, the town's popularity has yet to negatively impact its nearly picture-perfect setting in a mountain valley. There's heaps of quiet accommodation outside the main drag, a host of natural, lazy activities to keep visitors entertained and a vibrant art scene. And the town's Shan roots can still be seen in its temples, quiet backstreets and fun afternoon market.

Sights in Pai

Ban Santichon

Village in Pai

The cheesy photo ops, piped-in music, restaurants serving Yunnanese food, tea tastings, pony rides, tacky re-creation of the Great Wall of China and mountaintop viewpoint can make parts of Ban Santichon seem like a Chinese-themed Disneyland. But get past these and you'll find a living, breathing Chinese village, one well worth exploring. Located about 4km west of Pai.

Wat Phra That Mae Yen

Buddhist temple in Pai

This temple sits atop a hill and has terrific views overlooking the valley. To get there, walk 1km east from the main intersection in town to get to the stairs (353 steps) that lead to the top. Or, if you've got wheels, take the 400m sealed road that follows a different route.

Nam Tok Mo Paeng

Waterfall in Pai

Nam Tok Mo Paeng has a couple of pools that are suitable for swimming. The waterfall is about 8km from Pai along the road that also leads to Wat Nam Hoo – it's a long walk, but it's suitable for a bike ride or short motorcycle trip.

Phuket

First, let's get the pronunciation right. The 'h' in Phuket (ภูเก็ต) is silent. And then remember that this is the largest Thai island, so you rarely feel surrounded by water. But that means there is space for everyone. Phuket offers such a rich variety of experiences – beach-bumming, culture, diving, fabulous food, hedonistic or holistic pleasures – that visitors are spoilt for choice.

Of course, the white-sand beaches that ring the southern and western coasts are the principal draw, along with some of the finest hotels and spas in Thailand. Each beach is different, from the upmarket resorts of Surin and Ao Bang Thao, to family-oriented Rawai, or the sin city of Patong, home of hangovers and go-go girls. But there's also the culturally rich east-coast capital Phuket Town, as well as wildlife sanctuaries and national parks in the north. With so many options, you may just forget to leave.

Sights in Phuket

Big Buddha

Buddhist site in Phuket

Hours - 6am-7pm

Contact - http://www.mingmongkolphuket.com

Location - Phuket, Thailand

High atop the Nakkerd Hills, northwest of Chalong circle, and visible from half the island, the 45m-high Big Buddha sits grandly on Phuket's finest viewpoint. It's a tad touristy, but tinkling bells and flapping flags mean there's an energetic pulse. Pay your respects at the tented golden shrine, then step up to the glorious plateau, where you can peer into Kata's perfect bay, glimpse the shimmering Karon strand and, to the southeast, survey the pebble-sized channel islands of Chalong Bay.

Construction began on Big Buddha in 2007. He's dressed in Burmese alabaster, which isn't cheap. All in all, the price tag is around 100 million baht (not that anybody minds). Phuketians refer to the Big Buddha as Phuket's most important project in the last 100 years, which means a lot considering that construction on Phuket hasn't stopped for the last two decades.

From Rte 4021, follow signs 1km north of Chalong circle to wind 6km west up a steep country road, passing terraces of banana groves and tangles of jungle.

Laem Phromthep

Top choice viewpoint in Rawai

Location - Rte 4233, Rawai, Thailand

If you want to see the luscious Andaman Sea bend around Phuket, then come here, to the island's southernmost point. The cape is crowned by a mod lighthouse shaped like a concrete crab, and an evocative elephant shrine, so you'll want to stay a while. At sunset the hordes descend in luxury buses; if you crave privacy, take the faint fisherman's trail downhill to the rocky peninsula that reaches into the ocean and watch the sun drop in peace.

Hat Bang Thao

Beach in Ao Bang Thao

Beautiful 8km-long Hat Bang Thao is one of the longest beaches on Phuket. This dreamy slice of snow-white sand mixes midrange bungalows (at the south end), luxury resorts (in the middle) and not much else (north end). It's just asking for you to laze around on it and do nothing.

Pha Taem National Park

A long cliff named Pha Taem is the centrepiece of awesome but unheralded Pha Taem National Park (อุทยานแห่งชาติผาแต้ม), which covers 340 sq km along the Mekong River. From the top you get a bird's-eye view across the Mekong into Laos, and down below a trail passes prehistoric rock paintings.

The wilderness north of the cliff holds more ancient art, some awesome waterfalls (all flowing June to December), and scattered scattered rock fields known as Sao Chaliang, which are oddly eroded mushroom-shaped stone formations.

Many Thais come here for the sunrises. Pha Cha Na Dai cliff, which requires a high-clearance vehicle to reach, serves Thailand's first sunrise view. But Pha Taem cliff is only about one minute behind, and it has the country's first sunset view.

Conclusion

Thank you for reading my Thailand travel guide, I hope it has helped you.

Made in the USA
San Bernardino, CA
12 May 2018